"Tony Jeary's book could have been titled: *The Ultimate Presenter's Handbook*. It is loaded with practical advice, technical suggestions, and tools a professional presenter can begin to use immediately."
> —ZIG ZIGLAR
> The Zig Ziglar Corporation

Presentation skills are key to leadership! *Inspire Any Audience* is packed with specific solutions to help your presentation hit the bulls-eye. A must read for any leader to find the key to unlocking leadership potential.
> —JOHN C. MAXWELL, FOUNDER
> INJOY Ministries

"Every client who calls our International Speakers Bureau asks for a speaker who can INSPIRE their audience. If you speak to a handful of people or a worldful, this is the most essential book you can read. We will carry it in our international catalog. Bravo, Tony Jeary!"
> —DOTTIE WALTERS, President
> Walters International Speakers Bureau

"Everybody knows that to reach the top these days, you have to acquire the ability to speak in public. *Inspire Any Audience* will help one learn the skill."
> —TERRANCE J. MCCANN, Executive Director
> Toastmasters

"This is an outstanding guide for giving great presentations. It shows you how to inspire and excite an audience on any subject."
> —BRIAN TRACY, Author
> *Psychology of Achievement*

"It is a pleasure to acknowledge Tony Jeary and his fantastic work as a first-rate business consultant and personal trainer. . . . He is a man with a deep well of skills and a treasure trove of abilities found only in those few who have persevered to achieve great success."
> —DR. ROBERT H. SCHULLER
> *Hour of Power*

"Tony Jeary has mastered the art of inspiring an audience. Anyone who wants to improve their platform skills with real, proven ideas and techniques needs this book. I recommend it without hesitation."
> —PATRICK O'DOOLEY, CSP
> Former Board Member, National Speakers Association

I dedicate this work to my wife Tammy, my daughters Brooke and Paige, and my family for having the patience to support my dream, and to the many individuals who will read this work and hopefully gain insight from my years of study.

I gratefully acknowledge and appreciate everyone who has contributed to my life and this book.

INSPIRE ANY AUDIENCE

PROVEN SECRETS OF THE PROS
FOR POWERFUL PRESENTATIONS

BY
TONY JEARY

TRADE LIFE BOOKS
Tulsa, Oklahoma

Inspire Any Audience
Proven Secrets of the Pros for Powerful Presentations
ISBN 1-57757-026-X
Copyright © 1997 by Tony Jeary
High Performance Resources, Inc.
3001 LBJ Freeway, Suite 240
Dallas, TX 75234

Published by Trade Life Books, Inc.
P. O. Box 55325
Tulsa, OK 74155

Table of Contents

Foreword
by Zig Ziglar

I met Tony Jeary on a flight to Detroit as we were both on our way to see a mutual Fortune 500 client. After a short visit, we developed an immediate rapport. I soon realized that Tony was a dynamic individual with a lot to say and an effective way of saying it. Since that time, the relationship has grown, and I am excited about the opportunity to say nice things about him and the professional approach he takes to speaking, teaching, and training.

Whether we like it or not, people who articulate well, both privately and in front of a group, are generally perceived to be more intelligent and possess greater leadership qualities. There's no doubt about it, being able to speak effectively is vitally important whether the intent is to ask for a raise or persuade an individual or company to take a specific action.

Effective speaking skills can be especially valuable when you are called on to make an unexpected presentation. Such a situation can be intimidating, unpleasant, and potentially disastrous — or at least embarrassing! Nevertheless, if you occupy any type of leadership position in any organization, sooner or later such an occasion will arise. That's when preparation and pre-learned skills will come to the rescue and enable you to turn surprise to your advantage.

Tony Jeary is a master at handling these occasions, and more importantly, he has developed a system which is easy to learn, understand, and implement, so your own effectiveness will quickly improve. This improvement can help you get that raise, social acceptance, or recognition as a "doer" or at least a "comer." Confidence and effectiveness in front of a group are enormous assets.

Foreword

Tony Jeary has trained people on more than three continents in more than thirty countries, and developed effective speakers in each of them. In this book, he shares the knowledge he has acquired from hundreds of presentations developed over the years in a simple, easy-to-follow process. I hope that you will read this book, study it, mark it, and keep it handy as an ongoing reference source and reminder. This will certainly be a profitable investment of your time and provide personal, financial, and other benefits as well. It's good stuff!

—Zig Ziglar

Introduction

This book is about succeeding at the front of the room—any room!
The fact that you're reading it now indicates that you have a desire
to raise your level of expertise as a presenter. First, let me assure
you that your goal is attainable and second, let me congratulate you
for choosing this book to take you there. By reading and applying
the information and techniques I have outlined, I guarantee you will
become as comfortable at the front of any audience as you are right
now reading this book.

Why Inspire?

When I first began presenting, I knew I lacked *something* that truly
outstanding speakers have. Even as my skills grew, and my
audiences became more appreciative and responsive, I still sensed I
was missing something important.

That something, I would discover, is *inspiration*. Every great speaker
has the power to inspire. When some people speak, you can feel the
power of persuasion flowing through the room. The audience stirs.
They *buy-in* to what the speaker has to say. But it doesn't end there.
Truly great speakers do more than inspire their audiences on the
"feel good" level. Exceptional speakers manage to inspire their
audiences to *take action*. Audience members leave with the intention
of doing something—whether it is to sell new homes, apply new
techniques on the job, or reread the story of David and Goliath with
greater understanding.

This power to inspire has many names: charisma, persuasion, allure,
influence. But regardless of what we call it, it all comes down to one
thing—the ability to *move* people.

Without inspiration, there can be no actionable results. With it, you
will earn trust, buy-in, and critical acclaim. It will be said that you
possess that *certain something*.

I will make you this promise. If you follow the Seven Foundational Secrets® in this book and take an hour or so to learn the supporting materials, you will have at your disposal the power to *Inspire Any Audience*.

The book you now hold is a well-organized, easy-to-follow, easy-to-use tool. Simple, fun-to-read, and to-the-point, it's more than a how-to book. It's also a valuable reference guide that can be used every time you make a presentation — a lifetime resource, whether you are presenting in front of the PTA board or the board of directors. It's heavy on tips, pointers, worksheets, and checklists; and light on personal stories, philosophy, and other filler. It's "only the good parts." Your time is valuable. With that in mind, I have organized this book to ensure that you get exactly what you need.

> **Every great presentation contains a certain something that makes it excellent; and, if you could isolate it and repeat it, that certain something would make you a GREAT presenter.**

My Seven Foundational Secrets® of making a presentation are designed to earn the speaker 100 percent audience buy-in. They are the cornerstones of inspiring any audience.

Foundational Secret #1. *Funneling Process* — Simply put, this is a surveying tool. Its intent is to uncover your audience's hidden needs and wants, thus guaranteeing that your presentation is on target. By taking a few simple steps, you can clearly define your objectives and your message.

Foundational Secret #2. *Four Subconscious Tensions* — Understanding how to relieve the *four* subconscious tensions common to all audiences, will increase audience acceptance. Tension exists between (1) audience members and other audience members; (2) audience members and the presenter; (3) audience members and the materials the presenter provides for them; and (4) audience members and their environment.

Foundational Secret #3. *Trust* — Without trust there is no buy-in. I will show you how to use "trust transference" to ignite 100 percent buy-in every time you are in front of the room. By knowing your audience — what they like, who and what they trust — you can speed up the rapport process and bond more quickly and easily.

Foundational Secret #4. *Business Entertainment*™ — This is a must. If your audience isn't captivated, you can't be assured of their full attention and without their attention, you can't be effective. People like to have fun — think about why so many people (adults, too) flock to Disneyland. There are many forms of Business Entertainment™, some of which are described in this book. But for now, let's just call it the "fun factor."

Foundational Secret #5. *Verbal Surveying* — This is used to get feedback during your entire presentation — whether it is a 15-minute speech, a 3-day training seminar, or a 2-hour sales presentation. Simply by asking your audience, you can know how to pace your delivery and whether or not you are covering your subject in the right amount of detail. This allows you to adjust your presentation as you move through your material, ensuring that you stay on target.

Foundational Secret #6. *Targeted Polling* — You can decrease nervousness, relate to your audience, and establish advocates by taking advantage of opportunities to talk one-on-one with audience members. This can be done before you start, during breaks, and after your presentation. By polling or questioning a few people individually, you can accomplish a great deal. People like to be given individual attention, so make this opportunity work for you.

Foundational Secret #7. *Audience Closure* — Proper closure proves you have met and exceeded your audience's expectations. Executed properly, closure ensures that audience members leave your presentation as ambassadors for you and your subject matter.

Introduction

How to Use This Book

Inspire Any Audience: Proven Secrets of the Pros is designed for maximum effectiveness. It is divided into *four* chronological parts: (1) presentation development, which begins before the first word is uttered; (2) beginning of the presentation; (3) body of the presentation; and (4) conclusion of the presentation.

You can:

> Spend a few minutes thumbing through the book to get familiar with its flow.

> Address a specific need, such as dealing with nervousness, by going directly to a certain chapter or part.

> Read the book to understand the entire process.

> Study the Seven Foundational Secrets.

> Use *Inspire Any Audience* as a lifelong reference book.

> Use the last two chapters alone and get something more informative than most books offer—extra bang for your buck!

Extra Bang for Your Buck

Chapter 13, titled "Continuous Improvement," assembles a broad array of tools for self-evaluation. These tools are presented on separate pages so you can maximize each by simply making copies from the book.

I have also included my personal list of other products—the how-to books, tapes, and magazines I have used successfully. They are resources that you may not even know exist.

This chapter concludes with a list of my associates—professionals you might want to contact for personal coaching, in your hometown or an area nearby.

Chapter 14 is special to me. It features 18 perforated cards—on card stock. Tear out these pages and instantly, you have 18 special cards (in bulleted format) that contain the top secrets revealed throughout the text. These secrets, some simple, some not so simple, should save you hundreds of hours of research. They are the result of ten years spent collecting ideas to perfect my own presentations, plus many tips by other professional speakers. This chapter contains the real keys to improving your skill level as a presenter.

A Special Note: Even More Bang for Your Buck

I have designed this book to be user friendly, useful, and valuable. For those who like a little variety, the book is packed with boxed notes, quotes, and tons of checklists. In many chapters, you will find a mini-essay or two. I have called on a few of my colleagues to provide their unique perspectives and gathered extra materials to make sure I can *exceed* your expectations.

PART 1
Before Your Presentation

This chapter reveals:

➤ How to learn what your audience
   members think, want, and expect

➤ Why it is critical to identify your objectives
   before you begin to develop your presentation

➤ How to use the *Funneling Process*: five simple
   steps that will help you define your objectives
   before you begin to develop your presentation

1

Defining Your Objectives

JEARY THEORY ▬▬▬▬▬▬▬▬

To effectively present, you must first use a *Funneling Process* to identify your real objectives.

"Would you tell me please, which way I ought to go
from here?"
"That depends a good deal on where you want to
get to."

— Lewis Carrol, *Alice in Wonderland*

The Scene ...

You receive a call from your boss, who states that she would like
you to make a presentation since you have done such a good job
this year. Unfortunately, doing your job well does not make you a
trained presenter.

You volunteer to help with Sunday School activities. One of your
responsibilities is to lead a half-day seminar, but when you try to
write out your ideas, your mind goes blank.

You have an opportunity to make extra money in a way that has worked for many of your friends. However, you must give "opportunity presentations." In preparation, you collect a few bits of information from here and there, but you don't feel you have that certain something that makes presenting so easy for some people.

You must make a big presentation in your biology class. You know the material, but in the past, you haven't been prepared. This time you want to do better.

The Solution . . .

Information Goes in the Top Here and Is Funneled Down Through the Steps

1. **Determine the action.**
   - What action do I want my audience to take as a result of my presentation?
   - What must audience members know, say, and do differently when they leave my presentation?

2. **Define your audience.**
   - What are the skills, knowledge, and attitudes of my audience?
   - What are the positions represented in my audience?

3. **Brainstorm to determine needs.**
   - Your needs.
   - Your audience's needs.
   - Any third-party needs.

4. **Focus these needs into objectives.**
   - Work them into three or four *written* objectives, keeping in mind that audience members want practical, usable knowledge.
   - Keep objectives short.
   - Write out in one sentence what you want to accomplish. Refer to it often.

5. **Test your objectives mentally.**
   - Put yourself in your audience's shoes and check your objectives from their perspective.

Result = Core Objectives of Your Presentation

For all those scenes and hundreds more like them, I have developed a technique I call the *Funneling Process*. It takes all the things you might do—those hundreds of possibilities that daze and paralyze you like a deer caught in headlights—and funnels them down to a solid core of doable, reachable objectives. Most of us are good at accomplishing a handful of small chores once we know what they are. The problem with coming up with a new presentation—for the novices and masters alike—is deciding where we want to go and how we want to get there.

The *funneling process* will help you solve this problem.

Get Started by Using the Funneling Process to Define Your Objectives!

"With well-written, meaningful, and measurable objectives, the trainer has the course practically designed."

When you have your objectives on target, you can really inspire. When I'm starting to define objectives for a presentation, I use a proven process that I think you will find very valuable, whether you are in an auditorium talking with hundreds of people or in a business meeting with just a few in attendance!

—from *7 Steps to Building Better Training* by Martin M. Broadwell

Step 1. Determine the Action

The first step for developing clear objectives is to determine the action you want your audience to take. Three basic "actions" you can aim for when giving a presentation are the following:

1. **Changing an attitude.**
2. **Learning something (knowledge).**
3. **Attaining or perfecting a skill.**

For clarification, ask yourself:

➤ Do I wish to *change an attitude* among my listeners (a keynote address, motivating some associates or friends to action; a presentation at a manager's meeting; talking to a DARE group for teenagers; addressing the local PTA about school-lunch programs)?

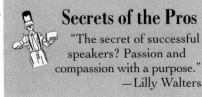

➤ **Do I wish to *impart some knowledge* to my listeners** (teaching Sunday School; coaching your child's baseball team; making a presentation to your sales staff)?

➤ **Do I wish to transfer a skill to my listeners** (teaching dance class; presenting to a hobby group or a rotary club; training fellow workers in your department)?

Once you've written down what you wish to accomplish, you're ready to define your audience.

Step 2. Define Your Audience

To create audience buy-in for your presentation, you must give your audience a good reason to listen to you. Otherwise, they may simply walk away. Their time is valuable, and that means that from your audience's viewpoint, your presentation has to answer a simple question: "What's in it for me?" But, in order to know what's in it for your audience—you must first know who your audience is.

Form a mental image of your audience, by completing the following checklist as soon as you schedule a presentation.

❏ Create a profile of the average audience member—include age, background, marital status, education, income, and job.

❏ Create a list of people your audience would likely admire—this can give you great insight.

❏ Talk with former attendees of the same types of presentations.

❏ Talk with former presenters who've addressed similar groups.

❏ Interview the client or event planner, if one is available.

❏ Request a list of likely audience members—then pre-poll them by calling in advance to see what they expect.

Follow these steps even when you think you know your audience. A clear understanding of who your audience is will provide a foundation for your entire presentation. Be thorough!

Although each audience you encounter is unique, I've discovered that all audiences share *seven subconscious desires*.

The Seven Subconscious Desires of Your Audience

Each member of your audience is a human being, who wants the following:

➤ **To belong**

➤ **To be respected**

➤ **To be liked**

➤ **To be safe**

➤ **To succeed**

➤ **To find romance**

➤ **To be inspired (enthused)**

Four Levels of Learning a Skill

1. **Unconscious Incompetence** — A time when the learner is not only unaware of skill, but moreover wouldn't be good at it if he were aware. A baby doesn't know about tying his shoe and couldn't tie it if he did.

2. **Conscious Incompetence** — The learner is aware of the skill, but nevertheless cannot perform it. A child becomes aware of Mom and Dad tying shoes, but can't do it.

3. **Conscious Competence** — The learner is aware of the skill and can consciously perform it. A child can tie his shoes, but sticks his tongue out because he has to think about it.

4. **Unconscious Competence** — The learner performs the skill without thinking about it. It becomes an automatic response. A child ties his shoes without thinking about it.

To begin Step 2: Ask yourself, "What are the skills, knowledge, and attitudes my audience possesses?"

Knowing your audience is crucial if you want to satisfy their needs. Too often, presenters skip this critical step. Don't make this mistake! Understand your audience's needs and the actions you want them to take to meet those needs even before you begin to develop your presentation. The time you invest now will pay big dividends later.

Presentation audiences are *active* — or at least they ought to be. Audience members generally come in one of *four* types. Explaining these four types and acknowledging the mental state (or tension) of audience members lets them know it's OK to be in whatever mind-set they're in. It also lets you relax and gives you credibility as a professional.

David Freeborn uses an interesting technique to address the four types of participants. He begins by saying, "Having presented seminars all over the world to all different types of people, I've discovered that participants typically fall into four basic categories or mental states.

First, we have ***The Prisoner.*** This is the person who does not particularly want to be here today. In fact, he would rather be *anywhere* other than indoors listening to another talk.

Recently, I was asked by one of my major clients to redesign a multimillion-dollar program for new franchisees. I took the assignment only after the client agreed I could have the time needed to survey the audience. I wanted to know everything I could about them — even though I had prepared work for this type of audience before. As a result of my survey efforts, I found out some things that were pertinent to the business at hand. I was able to understand the current needs of the audience and to create accurate objectives, thereby increasing the likelihood of a successful presentation.

How To Identify the Four Types of Audience Members

Prisoner—Look for crossed arms, both literally and figuratively.

Vacationer—Look for a good mood combined with an overrelaxed attitude.

Graduate—Look for frowns, rolling eyes, smug looks, and crossed arms.

Student—Look for smiles, enthusiastic nodding, and the merciful habit of laughing at your jokes.

Someone else made that decision for him by sending him to this seminar. It's OK if you're a *prisoner*. We welcome all *prisoners* because that only means you are not responsible for *being* here today . . . but you *are* responsible for what you take out of here! How many *prisoners* here today? Let me see a show of hands.

Next, we have *The Vacationer.* This is the person who volunteers to go to any seminar, figuring it's better to be in a meeting than at work, home, or wherever else he'd normally be. In other words, he's happy to be here, but for the wrong reasons. We're happy to have our *vacationers* on board today because they like to have fun, and we'll count on them to help us have a good time. How many *vacationers* do we have with us today?

Then there's *The Graduate.* This is the person who thinks he doesn't need to be here because he already knows this stuff. But we're glad to have the *graduates*, too, because this is the place for them to share all their knowledge and wisdom with others.

Finally, we have *The Student.* This is the attentive, hard-working, perfect audience member who wants to hear what we've come to say. He is eager to learn and share and, like a sponge, ready to absorb all he can to help him be more effective personally and professionally. We always welcome the *students*!"

Some audience members will represent a combination of these traits—but most will fit nicely into one of the categories.

Once you've done your basic audience research, fill out the form on page 42. This will give you a single audience reference page for developing your presentation.

Step 3. Brainstorm to Determine Needs

At this point, you have taken the following steps toward a successful presentation:

➤ **You've decided what action you wish your audience to take.**

➤ **You've begun to define what kind of audience members you'll have.**

When developing your objectives, keep in mind that all presentations must meet the needs of *three* distinct audiences. Success or failure is determined to one degree or another by how well your objectives meet the needs of these "audiences." The three audiences are listed below:

➤ **Attendees**. These are the lucky folks who get to hear you.

➤ **Any interested third parties**. This group can include but is not limited to clients, bosses, parents, friends, family, or anyone with a vested interest in how well your presentation turns out.

➤ **You**. The life of the party.

To use this information, try the following. Sit down at a table with three sheets of paper. At the top of the first, write: "The Audience." At the top of the second, write: "Third Parties." And on the third sheet, write: "Me." Under each heading, write down the essential needs that must be satisfied for that group—those things without which you might as well not even give the presentation. Next write down those things that are important—elements that would really make your presentation shine. Then write down the things that would make you a star—elements that anyone in any of the three audiences would consider to be above and beyond the call of duty.

Write freely—at this stage you're just brainstorming. Try to fill each page. If you fill one side of the sheet, turn it over and continue. Remember, this is raw resource material. You're simply trying to determine every possible need that you, your audience members, and any third parties might need to take home from your presentation. If you've gone off in numerous directions, written half-sentences, misspelled words, or come up with a bunch of unrelated ideas—congratulations! You're doing exactly what you ought to be doing—letting your brain "storm off" in any direction it chooses.

Once you've finished this step, set the paper aside and don't look at it for an hour or two—longer if possible. This will give you time to gain perspective on the raw material that will eventually become your focused objectives.

Secrets of the Pros

"When in doubt, take a survey."

—Dottie Walters

Step 4. Focus Needs into Objectives

Step 3—brainstorming your audience's needs—was the creative part of developing your objectives. Step 4 is the rational part. It requires taking all the ideas and raw material you've generated and focusing them into solid, clear objectives.

First, review the material again and focus on the *most important* needs on your list and possible ways of satisfying those needs. Once you've identified the most important needs, you will be ready to convert this raw material into objectives.

AUDIENCE WORKSHEET

What knowledge about my topic do they bring to the table?

_____

_____

_____

Will they be for me or against me? Why?

_____

_____

_____

Who are the people they most admire in their organizations and who are they most likely to admire outside their organizations?

_____

_____

_____

What things have worked with similar audiences in the past — and what things haven't?

_____

_____

_____

Why was I asked to present?

_____

_____

Begin by asking yourself the following questions:

➤ **Why am I giving this presentation?**

➤ **What's in it for my audience(s)?**

➤ **What is the purpose of the presentation? Is it:**

- **To inform?**

- **To instruct?**

- **To persuade?**

- **To entertain?**

- **All of the above**

➤ **What do I want my audience(s) to say after the presentation?**

➤ **What do I want my audience(s) to believe?**

➤ **What *specific* action do I want my audience(s) to take?**

Once you've answered these questions, you're prepared to write down your objectives. Do so in *three* short, concise sentences. These sentences—your objectives—should address the *what, how,* and *why* of your presentation:

➤ **WHAT will be the actual content of the presentation?**

➤ **HOW detailed will the information in the presentation be and HOW long will the presentation last?**

➤ **WHY will audience members wish to act when they leave the presentation?**

Your sentences should be as short and clear as possible. Avoid weak and vague phrases like, "To become familiar with five answers to Problem X...." Instead, use *action* words that

> ## Secrets of the Pros
>
> "I like to get my talk down to three or four 'big hit' things that people can take home with them—like the way I write. I think people fall asleep with lists. Whenever a speaker starts off with, 'Here are ten points I'm going to make . . .' I go into snoozeville."
>
> —Dr. Ken Blanchard

43

give clear directions: "To identify the five steps needed to resolve Problem X." The clearer and more specific your three objectives, the easier it will be for you to develop your presentation.

Again, limit yourself to *three sentences;* anything more is too much to try to accomplish in a single presentation. It's tempting but don't give in! An overpacked presentation creates an overwhelmed audience, resulting in a loss of interest during your presentation and almost zero retention. Providing just the right amount of information begins with the creation of clear and focused objectives.

Step 5. Test Your Objectives Mentally

Once you've written down your three objectives, test them by putting yourself in your audience's shoes. Remember, each audience member wants to know, "What's in it for me?" To make

One True Sentence

Many presenters like to write a mission statement as part of their objectives. A mission statement is one sentence that sums up the presentation and what it will accomplish:

"To provide an entertaining atmosphere for learning sales techniques that will increase audience members' product awareness and increase their income."

You should strongly consider trying to sum up your presentation in one single sentence and then refer back to it repeatedly. It keeps your eyes on the prize and lets you remain focused on the big picture while working out the details.

> I've always used a basic preparation format for developing presentation objectives. I imagine myself planning a trip.
>
> 1. What is the **destination** (the conclusion or action required)?
>
> 2. What is the **route** (amount of detail and information)?
>
> 3. What **speed** do I need to drive?
>
> 4. Why am **I driving**?
>
> 5. Why are we **going on the trip**?
>
> I wouldn't go to Disneyland without a few clear reasons and directions. Why would I give a presentation with less?
>
> —Fred Collins

sure your objectives address this question, ask yourself the following questions:

➤ **Are my objectives clear?**

➤ **Do I know *what* I want to accomplish; *how* I want to accomplish it; and *why* I want to accomplish it?**

➤ **Have I used *action* words that describe what my presentation will do?**

➤ **Do my objectives give my audience members a good reason to listen?**

Though objectives must address your needs and the needs of any third party, the most important group to address is your immediate audience. Make sure your objectives work for them.

Secrets of the Pros

"A clear picture of desired outcomes is essential to success in meeting, training, and other communications. If you don't know what you want, you won't get what you need."

—George Lowe

Keep It Simple!

> "The art of art, the glory of expression and the sunshine of the light of letters is simplicity."
>
> —Walt Whitman
> "Leaves of Grass"

> "Keep It Simple, Stupid."
>
> —Anonymous

Ok, so there are elegant and not-so-elegant ways of saying the same thing as seen in the previous two quotations. But Walt Whitman and our anonymous poet both offer the same truth: The simple way is usually the best way to get a job done. There's something marvelous about solving a complex problem with a simple solution—and the same is true for any presentation.

When creating your objectives, be reasonable in your expectations of yourself and your audience: go for the goal you can achieve in the real, not the ideal, world. When writing down those objectives, strive for clarity and simplicity; this creates an impression of confidence and precision, while relieving the audience of work.

And when addressing your audience, use the simple, plain, and powerful language of everyday talk. Remember, you want them to want to have you back. Make your presentation memorable by trading in pompous complexity for saintly simplicity.

Secrets of the Pros

"Move them to make a decision every time you stand up."

—Tim Salladay

In Summary

Your objectives are the signposts, not the destination of your presentation. Would you go on a long trip without at least glancing occasionally at the road signs? Probably not. But too many presenters jump in and start developing the nitty-gritty details of a presentation before they've carefully considered where they're going and why. This results in an unfocused, confusing presentation that in a "best-case scenario" gets reworked, and in a "worst-case scenario" fails.

Avoid both by creating clear objectives at the outset, then delivering them in your presentation!

Very Important Points To Remember

✔ Clear objectives are the bedrock of a good presentation — without them, a presentation lacks focus, direction, and value.

✔ Create objectives by following the steps outlined in the *funneling process*.

✔ Objectives should be short, well-focused, and answer three questions: *What* will you present? *How* will you present it? and *Why* should the audience listen?

✔ When developing your objectives, know your immediate audience, and help them answer one basic question: "What's in it for me?"

Fill in Your Favorite Tips from the Chapter

✔ _____
_____

✔ _____
_____

✔ _____
_____

✔ _____
_____

✔ _____
_____

✔ _____
_____

This chapter reveals:

➤ How to build a three-dimensional outline, (3-D Outline™) from your objectives

➤ How to develop a complete presentation from beginning to end

➤ How to rehearse what you have developed

2

Developing and Rehearsing Your Presentation

JEARY THEORY

To build a great presentation, you start by building a great outline that includes timing along with the whats, whys, and hows of the presentation—then rehearse with it.

"It isn't the will to win that's important. Everyone has the will to win. What's important is the will to *prepare* to win."

— Bobby Knight

The Scene . . .

You've decided to take the services your small independent firm offers and present them in person to prospective clients. You already know what your top three objectives are because you used the *Funneling Process* outlined in chapter 1 of this book. Now you have your objectives lined out and your challenge is to turn those objectives into a well-prepared, flexible, and entertaining presentation.

Secrets of the Pros
"No practice —
No Improvement!"
— Daron Powers

The Solution . . .

You must turn your objectives into a presentation. Proceed through the two-part process outlined below. Part one will take you from blank paper to a full-fledged presentation. Part two will show you how to maximize your time by detailing effective ways to rehearse and hone your presentation.

Secrets to Developing Your Presentation

1. **Start with the top three objectives you developed using the** *Funneling Process* **from chapter 1.** Your presentation will be built around these.

2. **Define your limitations with the following questions:**
   - ➤ *How* much time will I have to prepare?
   - ➤ *How* much time will I have to speak?
   - ➤ *What* kind of room will I be speaking in?
   - ➤ *What* is my budget: large, small, or nonexistent?
   - ➤ *What* equipment will be available to me?

3. **Build a 3-D Outline™.** It should have at least four columns with the following headings, running left to right:
   TIME   WHAT   WHY   HOW

4. **Decide on, then apply, a logical sequence to your presentation.** Some of the more widely used sequences are the following:
   - ➤ Past to present
   - ➤ Priority (relative importance of various topics)
   - ➤ Pain to pleasure
   - ➤ Categorical
   - ➤ Comparison and contrast
   - ➤ Advantages and disadvantages
   - ➤ Ideal vs. reality

5. **Pare back any point that takes more than 15 minutes to explain.** Keep your pacing fast and your ideas simple.

6. **Identify and secure the best tools your budget will allow.**

7. **Brainstorm and review your material with other developers, if possible.**

Start with Crystal-Clear Objectives

Begin developing your presentation by reviewing the sheet that summed up your top three objectives in chapter 1. These will drive the creative process. Objectives are as varied as presentation topics themselves, but examples of objective summations could look like this:

For a presentation on Freudian psychology:

1. **Identify the top three concepts for this year's psychological convention: the ego, the id, and the super-ego.**

2. **Ensure that the audience buys-in to the three concepts and retains at least one major point about each.**

3. **Excite the audience about these three ideas and inspire in them a desire to learn more.**

For a presentation on the relevance of the biblical story "David and Goliath," use the following steps:

➤ **Create excitement among listeners for this and other Bible stories.**

➤ **Make sure listeners understand and retain the reading of David and Goliath as a lesson on perseverance and determination.**

➤ **Instruct listeners in the notion of "interpretation" and what it means to them.** As you close, ensure that they have an understanding of why stories like this matter to them.

Presentation differs from other modes of communication in the following way: you *present* your objectives by delivering **short and easy-to-memorize** pieces of information. This is one of the most important ways a presentation differs from a book. Always remember that presentation audiences want:

➤ **Practical, usable knowledge.**

➤ **Information presented in an easy-to-remember format.**

A writer's job is to deliver all the details—the rules and their exceptions, the research, the analysis, the facts, the figures, and the data for the reader to digest and use at some future time. The presenter's job is to think through that material and create something that will impact the listeners now. A presentation is immediately actionable and, if closed properly, includes *a call to action.* This action orientation is accomplished partly because the presentation is delivered in clearly delineated and easily digestible parts. These parts or segments include:

➤ **Introduction**

➤ **Body**

- **subsection one**
- **subsection two**
- **subsection three**
(and so on)

➤ **Close**

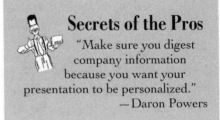

Secrets of the Pros

"Make sure you digest company information because you want your presentation to be personalized."
— Daron Powers

No rocket science here. The trick is to make sure each part and each subsection of your presentation does the job it's meant to do. For now, it's important to remember that a presentation is made up of *sections* joined together by *transitions.* By dividing material into sections, your mind can digest and sort it better. Think of a phone number in three sections: area code, prefix, and four numbers. (For an in-depth discussion of the various *sections* of your presentation, what they ought to accomplish, and how to reach those goals, see the appropriate chapter — Introduction: chapter 4; Body: chapter 10; Close: chapter 12.)

What Then?

The first concrete step in developing a presentation is to decide *what you're going to say.* This is where most people get stuck, usually because there is such a variety of information you can present, directions you can take, and approaches you can use. There's just too much to choose from, and that can be overwhelming. The best way to ease this panic is to sort through the possibilities. Do this by filling out a worksheet I like to call a "presentation work order" (See the next page).

This should give you a realistic idea of what your limitations are, and a clear idea of your limitations will help you sort out what you can and cannot say. Once you know how much time you have to prepare and how much time you'll have to deliver your presentation, you will be able to visualize the path your presentation will eventually take. Bring it further into focus by creating a 3-D Outline™.

THE PRESENTATION WORK ORDER

Title of presentation _____

Date of presentation _____

How much time do I have to prepare? _____

How much time will I have to speak? _____

What kind of room will I be speaking in?

❑ Conference room   ❑ Living room

❑ Boardroom   ❑ Other _____

❑ Classroom

How many people will I be speaking to? _____

What type of financial budget is available?

❑ Large budget—lots of money, as in   <u>$ Let's do it right!</u>
  "Money is no (big) object."

❑ Small budget—money is available $_____
  but definitely an object.

❑ No budget—money isn't an object $ _____0_____
  because there isn't any to spend.

What type of equipment will be available?

❑ Flip chart(s)?   ❑ Overhead projector?

❑ Tape player?   ❑ VCR and monitor?

❑ Advanced presentation   ❑ Chairs and tables?
  hardware and software?

❑ Other _____

What type of equipment do I need to provide/rent?_____

_____

What about handouts? _____

_____

3-D Outline™

The difference between a standard outline and a 3-D Outline™ is that the latter indicates not only what you want to say but also when, why, and how to say it. It is an indispensable part of any presentation preparation.

A 3-D Outline™ or matrix, lets you see the "big picture" and allows you to begin sorting through the material you'll have to produce right away. On the following pages, I have provided a simple blank sheet for filling in your "first draft" presentations. The first two pages show a sample matrix created by two imaginary presenters Sigmund and Carl, who are preparing a team presentation. The third page shows a complex matrix, designed for a longer presentation with lots of material and more than one presenter.

These complex 3-D Outlines™ can be tailor-made (on a computer or by hand) to fit your presentation's own specifications, and they allow you to make the most of that valuable commodity—time. Remember to start with a simple matrix (like the one that follows) so you can visualize the "big picture."

> **Secrets of the Pros**
>
> "There are always three speeches, for every one you actually gave: The one you practiced ... the one you gave ... the one you wish you gave!"
> —Dale Carnegie

Complete each column with the following information:

➤ **TIME:** This column records the amount of time you'll have to cover each segment of your presentation (e.g., your introduction, your agenda, your top three points, etc.).

➤ **WHAT:** This column identifies each segment of your presentation. At this stage, you will want to include only the main points you can cover in your allotted *time*.

➤ **WHY:** This column is for recording the reason *why* you have chosen *what* you will say and the *time* you will spend saying it.

➤ **HOW:** This column includes the method of delivering (e.g., video, overheads, role-plays).

Condensed 3-D Outline™

Title of presentation: _____

Date of draft: _____

Objectives of presentation:

- _____
- _____
- _____

TIME Allotted	WHAT	WHY	HOW
5 min.	Welcome	Relaxation	Talk
7 min.	Show Opening Video	Vary Media	Video
10 min.	Icebreaker	Excitement	Game
30 min.			
15 min.			
10 min.	Break		

The sample matrix above will get you started.

Developing Your Presentation

55

SAMPLE 3-D OUTLINE™

Title of Presentation: Ego, Super-ego, and Id: Today's Mind

Objectives:

1. Identify the top three concepts for this year's psychological convention: the ego, the id, and the super-ego.

2. Ensure that the audience buys-in to the three concepts and retains at least one major point about each.

3. Excite the audience about these three ideas and inspire in them a desire to learn more.

TIME	WHO*	SEGMENT	WHAT	WHY	HOW
3 min.	CARL		Welcome	Grab attention and revel commitments	Intro
7 min.	CARL		Show opening video	Keep interest	Video
10 min.	SIGMUND	I N T R O	Icebreaker; paper-tear activity	Involve audience	Game
30 min.	SIGMUND		Introduce key concepts for the day: • EGO • ID • SUPER-EGO	Introduce important concepts to learn	Overheads
3 min.	CARL		Present day's agenda: where we're going next		
10 min.			Break	Refresh audience	

* Note how this organizer has included a column for extra speakers and a column for reminding himself which segment he is currently delivering.

Decide on a Logical Sequence for Your Presentation

Take a look at everything you have in front of you. By now you've determined what type of audience you have. You've completed your objectives. You've filled in the presentation work order, and you have established what will and won't be part of your presentation. Now, you must decide how you're going to sequence the material.

The sequences below are the most common arrangements for organizing the material you'll present. You can use just one or mix-and-match them to suit the specific type of material or audience you're dealing with—remember, variety is the spice of life.

Past to present: This method presents material chronologically. It works well when you need to cover historical periods or trace the development of a product, position, or concept.

Priority: This method presents material in the order of its relative importance.

Advantages and disadvantages: This method presents a point in such a way as to show its up side and down side. This is especially good for presenting controversial material or when presenting to inform an individual or group before a decision is made.

Pain to pleasure: This method takes the audience through an unfortunate but correctable situation along with a list of possible solutions.

Categorical: This method requires the creation of categories for your material. You might organize your material into sections such as "Features and Benefits," "Competitive Comparisons," or "Heroes and Villains." The categorical arrangement is good when you have a lot of complex points that need to be presented simply.

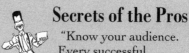

Secrets of the Pros

"Know your audience. Every successful salesperson alive today goes into a potential customer's office prepared, by knowing who he will be talking to."

—Sherry Boecher

Experiment with these arrangements and, if you can, use more than one for a presentation that lasts more than an hour. Different

Developing Your Presentation

segments can be presented using different sequences. Your introduction might employ *Past to Present;* then your opening segment might launch off in a *Priority* sequence. You might close with *Pain to Pleasure.* The key

is to have fun and create variety! Your audience will appreciate it.

On the following page is a large matrix on which to record a long (one full day or longer) presentation.

3-D OUTLINE™

Title of Presentation: _____

Objectives:

- _____
- _____
- _____

Time	Who	What	Why	How

✻ Include this category when featuring more than one speaker,

Starting to generate a lot of paper? Visit your local office supply and pick up a plastic-covered three-ring binder. Title it (especially the spine) with your presentation's title, date it, and begin to file the worksheets and pages you generate. This will provide you with an easy-to-access record.

REHEARSING YOUR PRESENTATION

What Is Effective Rehearsal?

Having a solid outline for your presentation is absolutely necessary, but it does not complete your preparation. The most critical step is rehearsal. A great presenter always appears to be comfortable, relaxed, and in control. This relaxed, controlled demeanor is not so much the result of natural poise as it is effective rehearsal. Many think they are rehearsing by reading notes, studying subject mate-rial, or memorizing parts of the presentation. All of this helps, but these steps alone do not constitute effective rehearsal.

> Effective rehearsal means making the best of your preparation time to become comfortable, relaxed, and in control — both mentally and physically. It also means anticipating and avoiding troubles before they happen.

Without effective rehearsal you run the risk of undoing all the hard work you've put into your presentation.

Seven Simple Steps to Rehearse Your Presentation

1. Mentally walk through your presentation using the 3-D Outline™/matrix.
2. Use 3x5 cards of key points, times, and directions while rehearsing.
3. Rehearse with audio or videotape practice sessions. Study your expressions and tone.
4. Rehearse in front of someone (associates, spouse, friend).
5. Rehearse with the equipment you'll use (pointer, flip chart, overheads).
6. Know your room: walk the room before your presentation at the actual rehearsal site.
7. Sit in an audience seat to get a feel for the room.

The Mental Walk-Through

Great athletes all know the importance of a mental walk-through. After the 1972 Olympics, Mark Spitz was asked to account for his great success as a swimmer. He explained that he had imagined himself swimming every lap of every event months before the event took place. Great skiers, boxers, runners, and football players tell similar stories. If imagination works in sports, the most physical of all endeavors, it can do wonders for your performance at the front of the room.

To begin your mental walk-through, determine how long you will speak and how you might begin. Then proceed to the next segment. This is different from memorizing your presentation, which is always a bad idea. (See chapter 4.) The mental walk-through familiarizes you with the flow of your presentation. Do the following exercise until you become familiar with all the parts of your presentation. Then do it some more.

1. Walk through each step.

2. Imagine your successful introduction of each step and point.

3. Go through to the end each time. Repeat.

Use 3x5 Cards

Write down three to seven key phrases on each 3x5 card. Organize the cards in the chronology of your presentation. The cards will remind you of key phrases and provide you with a place to record ideas, transitions, and other material that will make your flow of words seem natural and relaxed. Just the act of writing on the cards will help you solidify phrases and points in your head.

Secrets of the Pros

"Practice as often as you can in front of as many people as possible prior to the 'big presentation.'"

— Paul Boitmann

Once you've rehearsed with the 3x5 cards a few times, something magical begins to happen. You begin to form a mental picture of the cards. In a best case scenario, you'll carry a mental image of these cards into your presentation. But even if you don't, you can carry the actual cards—they're small, inconspicuous, and you've rehearsed with them. Remember to number your cards in case they are dropped.

Practice in Front of Someone — and, if Possible, Use Video!

Most people—and highly experienced speakers and presenters are sometimes the worst culprits—fail to take the crucial step of practicing out loud in front of people. Remember, what sounds good on paper (and even in your head) doesn't always work in front of an audience. Any problem is simple enough to fix when a friend, spouse, or coworker catches it three days before you present.

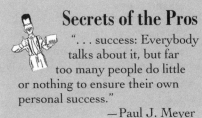

Secrets of the Pros

"... success: Everybody talks about it, but far too many people do little or nothing to ensure their own personal success."
—Paul J. Meyer

Practicing in front of people also gets you through the mechanics of moving from mental rehearsal to physical rehearsal. A lot can happen to a word as it travels from your brain to your mouth. It's best for any mishaps to occur on the testing ground and not on the racetrack!

Another trick is to videotape yourself—again and again. There's no replacement for understanding how you look when speaking. Watch the tape to see:

➤ **How well the words and transitions flow.**

➤ **How comfortable you appear with the material.**

➤ **How your posture, pronunciation, and word speed measure up.**

➤ **How you can make *your presentation better.***

Practice Makes Perfect

Your face is one of your most important presentation tools. Become familiar with it and practice using it the way musicians practice with their instruments. Use the mirror regularly! Be sure to:

➤ **Get to know what your face really looks like.**

➤ **Practice smiling naturally.**

➤ **Know how your expression appears when you are: happy, angry, nervous, tired, etc.**

Rehearse with the Equipment You Will Be Using

It's always best to rehearse with the equipment you intend to use. (For an in-depth discussion of presentation tools and how to use them, turn to chapter 10.) If you plan to use flip charts, practice with flip charts. If you plan to use videotape and overheads, rehearse with them. Equipment can cause mechanical and logistical headaches. Get used to the mechanics in the right way and at the right time—ahead of schedule. Actors do dress rehearsals—so should you!

The Last Hours Before Your Presentation

There's no replacement for rehearsing in the actual room in which you will be making your presentation. If that's not practical, rehearse in a similar room or set up a room in your house as similar as possible to your presentation room. Always try to get into the actual room to get acclimated before the presentation.

There are two reasons to do this. First, you need to physically know the space—where the light switches, outlets, doors, tables, chairs, cords, or rough spots in the rug are located—anything that might cause you to fall flat on your face (figuratively and literally). Equally important, you must make the room mentally yours. You're close to being fully prepared, now drive home your preparation by walking through the room. Know every corner of it from a presenter's perspective.

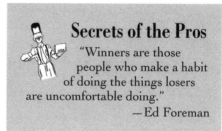

Secrets of the Pros

"Winners are those people who make a habit of doing the things losers are uncomfortable doing."

—Ed Foreman

Finally, do something few presenters ever do—sit in the audience seats! Know how the room will look and feel to your audience members. Can everyone see the front of the room and hear what is said without straining? Is the seating too cramped? Do the lighting and room temperature provide a comfortable environment? In a few short hours, your audience members will become the most important people in your life. Find out how to make them comfortable.

CHECKLIST FOR EFFECTIVE REHEARSAL

Well before your presentation:

Prepare and mentally walk through:

❑ Your 3-D Outline™

❑ Each section of your presentation

❑ Your 3x5 cards

Rehearse in front of :

❑ Other people

❑ Video camera

❑ Mirror

Just before your presentation:

Locate and find out how to operate:

❑ Electrical outlets

❑ Lighting controls

❑ Volume controls for room sound

❑ Window-blind cords

Locate the following:

❑ Restrooms

❑ Telephones

❑ Stairs and elevators

❑ Smoking areas

Comments:

_____

_____

_____

_____

_____

_____

_____

Very Important Points To Remember

✔ Begin developing your presentation with a clear understanding of your limitations and then fill out a "presentation work order" to develop realistic expectations.

✔ Create a 3-D Outline™ to determine where you're going.

✔ Logically order the material of your presentation by mixing and matching sequences in your presentation's subsections.

And remember:

✔ The most important three steps to take for an effective presentation are:

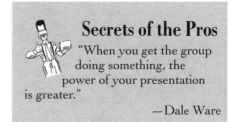

Secrets of the Pros

"When you get the group doing something, the power of your presentation is greater."

—Dale Ware

➤ **Rehearse**

➤ **Rehearse**

➤ **Rehearse**

✔ Always take time to sit in the audience seats as part of your rehearsal. Knowing how the world looks to them will help you become a superior presenter.

Fill in Your Favorite Tips from the Chapter

✔ _____

_____

✔ _____

_____

✔ _____

_____

✔ _____

_____

✔ _____

_____

✔ _____

_____

Developing Your Presentation

This chapter reveals:

➤ Proven methods for calming the jitters

➤ Proven methods for gaining a confident state of mind

➤ Tips on how to bond with your audience

➤ Tips on how to make enthusiasm rise from the ashes of your nervousness

3

Nervous to Natural

JEARY THEORY

Nervousness comes from the fear of the unknown. Discover the sources of your nervousness and you can conquer them.

"It all changed when I realized I'm not the only one on the planet who's scared. Everyone else is too."

—Stan Dale

Secret Steps for Going from Nervous to Natural

1. Know what you're talking about.

Thorough preparation equals total confidence. Prepare, and then rehearse, rehearse, rehearse! Understand that your audience wants you to succeed.

Practice meaningfully—the way you'll actually deliver your presentation. (Refer to chapter 2 for the best rehearsal techniques.)

Secrets of the Pros

"A man's doubts and fears are his worst enemies."
—William Wrigley, Jr.

2. Be yourself.

Use your own natural speaking style. Don't try to be someone you're not.

3. Psyche yourself up—use positive self-talk.

Visualize success: picture your audience applauding for you at the end of your presentation, then work toward it.

4. Work on your body's physical reaction to nerves.

Do stretching, isometrics, or some other exercise to relieve physical nervousness.

Take deep breaths to control breathing.

Pausing: proper pausing conveys relaxation and confidence.

5. Bond with your audience.

Keep the audience on your side.

Pick two or three friendly faces; speak to them in your opening and feed off their positive energy.

Extra Tip: Get a good night's sleep before your presentation.

The Scene . . .

You have been instructed to lead a presentation at the quarterly sales meeting next month. You know your material well—your boss knows that. But you're terrified of speaking in front of people.

You've prepared and rehearsed your presentation on local safety issues to be delivered to the local commerce committee until it seems like you could deliver it in your sleep. Your 3-D Outline™ is as solid as Plymouth Rock. You look great on your videotape. But as soon as you stand up to rehearse in front of two or three of your friends, your mind goes blank. You have to look at your rehearsal cards, which confuse you even more. Before you know it, it seems like you haven't prepared at all. If you can't

> **Secrets of the Pros**
>
> "Do what you know, what you live, what you believe. Doing overcomes fear every time!"
>
> —Ed Foreman

stay calm in front of three or four friends, how will you ever manage to deliver your presentation in front of a room full of strangers?

You have to speak in about one hour. You've been reviewing your notes, avoiding coffee, and trying to psyche yourself up for success. But you're so nervous that your hands are shaking and your knees feel weak. What can you do to get your body under control?

The Solution . . .

A single system is needed to address all the different ways in which you feel nervous, including the physical manifestations of nervousness—butterflies in the stomach, dry mouth, wet palms—and the mental manifestations—negative self-talk, fear, and apprehension. In fact, an ideal solution would be to take all the energy you're wasting on being nervous and funnel it back into the presentation in the form of enthusiasm.

You're Not Alone

There is both good news and bad news about nervousness—the good news is that everyone feels it. The bad news is that everyone feels it. The difference between those who appear to be free of nervousness and

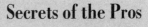

Secrets of the Pros

"Everyone has butterflies in their stomach. The only difference between a pro and an amateur is: the pro has the butterflies in formation!"

— Zig Ziglar

those who suffer its devastating effects is *control*. When you see someone who seems relaxed, confident, and natural standing at the front of the room, it's because that person has mastered the techniques of keeping nervousness under control!

Speaking in public is the number-one fear of people in America—if you conquer it, you will have a great competitive edge!

Step 1: Conquer Nervousness: Know What You're Talking About

The single best way to fight nervousness is to be well prepared. Nervousness is rooted in psychological stress (fear of failure) that manifests itself in physical symptoms (fast pulse, shallow breathing, dry mouth, sweaty palms, sick stomach, strange voice, and jittery knees). The bottom line is that preparation pays big dividends. If you're well prepared, and still feel nervous, your preparation will help reduce your nervousness once you begin to speak.

Top Ten Fears Among Americans
1. Speaking before a group
2. Heights
3. Insects and bugs
4. Financial problems
5. Deep water
6. Sickness
7. DEATH (!!!)
8. Flying
9. Loneliness
10. Dogs

From *The Book of Lists*

This section of the book and its tips deal with nerves at all stages of the game—a month before, the night before, or an hour before your presentation. If you've followed the easy steps to preparation and rehearsal outlined in chapters 1 and 2, you've probably got a whole binder full of papers. The night before your presentation, *take action* by reviewing these notes and running the checklists you've prepared. This will help reduce nervousness.

Professional speaker David Peoples, author of *Presentations Plus*, has this to say about reducing nervousness:

Knowing that you have done your homework and are well prepared will provide you with a peaceful confidence as soon as you get a few words out of your mouth. You can jump-start this process by getting the audience involved quickly.

Thorough preparation equals total confidence. Prepare, and then rehearse, rehearse, rehearse! Understand that your audience wants you to succeed!

"The single most effective thing you can do for sweaty palms is *rehearse*. The second most effective thing you can do for sweaty palms is *rehearse*. Guess what the third most effective thing is?"

Step 2: Be Yourself

Don't even think about trying to be someone you're not. You might see a great presenter a week before your presentation—someone who has a Don Rickles style of

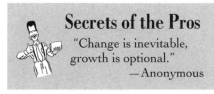

Secrets of the Pros

"Change is inevitable, growth is optional."
—Anonymous

poking jokes at the audience or someone who runs back and forth and makes things up as she goes. The audience may love these folks and you might be tempted to imitate them. Take it from me—don't.

Audiences see through pretense. You have enough to worry about when you're giving a presentation—don't add to your burden by trying to do imitations. The following is a partial list of what can go wrong when you try to be someone you are not:

➤ **You can make a poor first impression and then have nothing to fall back on.**

➤ **Your humor may be strained because it is not natural—not from your heart, like all good humor. Unnatural humor ranges from dry and boring to utterly disastrous.**

➤ **Your eye contact will be weak because you'll be busy focusing on being something you're not.**

Nervous to Natural

The Only Time To Be Something Other than Yourself

Acting confident and enthusiastic actually helps to create confidence and enthusiasm. If you are passionate about what you are presenting and believe in what you're doing, it will be easy for you to deal with your nerves when you follow the tips in this book. Don't imitate the actions or habits of other speakers—imitate only their confidence by emulating their preparation.

Being Yourself Can Be Humorous

Professional facilitator Myra Ketterman tells a story about her 17-year-old son, Jared, with whom she has a very close relationship. One day when Myra left home, she called back wanting to chat with Jared one more time before hopping on the plane. Jared answered the phone with his usual sweet southern "Hello," and Myra said, "Jared, I sure do love you." Jared replied, "Hey, I love you too! Who is this?" He was a bit surprised to discover it was Mom and follow-up to that conversation definitely took place!

Everyone in her audience was able to relate to the humor in her story. Many were parents of teenagers, or could at least remember being 17 years old themselves. It's another great way to break the ice and move into feeling more natural.

➤ You will invariably lack conviction and enthusiasm.

➤ The audience will resent your attempt or be embarrassed for you.

Conclusion: Be yourself!

"What if my natural self is a nervous wreck?" you ask. Great question! Proceed to step three and let's get to work fixing up that nervous wreck.

Step 3: Psyche Yourself Up Effectively: Your Mind's Reaction

It may or may not be in words, but we give ourselves messages and commands constantly. In fact, we do it so often, we don't even think about it. This constant, often wordless, dialogue is known in the presentation business as "self-talk." All too often we let our *self-talk* become negative without realizing it. Examples of negative *self-talk* include:

➤ They're gonna hate me.

➤ I'll never get prepared in time.

➤ I'm just too nervous to stand up in front of those people.

➤ Last time I stood up in front of this group, I dropped all my files—what if it happens again?

This negative *self-talk* sends exactly the wrong message — it psyches us out. Examples of positive *self-talk* include:

> Visualize success: picture your audience applauding for you at the end of your presentation, then work toward that goal.

➤ **The audience is going to love me because *they really want me to succeed*.** (See sidebar below.)

➤ **If I take a deep breath and concentrate, I will be *more than prepared* on time.**

➤ **Following the steps to reducing nerves in *Inspire Any Audience: Proven Secrets of the Pros* will help me overcome nervousness and make me confident and competent in front of any audience.** All I have to do is *be myself.*

➤ **Last time I stood up in front of this group, I dropped my files, but I also got the audience laughing *with* me by the end**

FACT: Your Audience Really Wants You to Succeed

Think back to the last time you were at a circus or saw one on TV. Imagine now that you are in that audience at the circus and far above you the trapeze artists are working their magic, with the greatest of ease. Fun, right? Now the trick gets harder as the trapeze artist's crew removes the net from beneath her. You tense up, maybe sit on the edge of your seat, and glance at the people around you. In short, you're nervous. The stunt proceeds and the daring young lady flies from her bar out into empty air. The audience gasps, and then her partner swoops into the picture and snags her back to safety — and everyone breathes a sigh of relief.

Why? Because deep down, we want her to succeed. *Your* audience is the same. For the most part, they are nearly as anxious as you. Always remind yourself of this simple but powerful fact: *my audience wants me to succeed.* This is true of even a fairly hostile audience and is probably due an inborn tendency to enjoy the spectacle of success.

of my presentation. I'll focus on the positive outcome, not a negative incident.

If you can't help but think negatively, try this. Visualize failure and then fabulous success. Which is more fun? Another technique to calm jitters is to put things into perspective. I "catastrophize" and ask myself, "What's the worst possible thing that can happen?" In the big scheme of things, the worst possible thing that could happen during my presentation probably isn't that terrible anyway. It is only a blip on the radar scope of eternity. Think positively!

The Mind-Body Connection

Self-talk works for you (or against you) because nervousness is really your body's natural response to stressful situations. Scientists believe that these feelings date back to our pre-historic ancestors, who were instinctively programmed for

Secrets of the Pros

"The human mind is a wonderful thing—it starts working the minute you're born and never stops until you get up to speak in public."
—Roscoe Drummond

"fight or flight" when faced with stress in the wild—maybe in the form of a saber-toothed tiger or a big brown bear. Today, when we're faced with the unknown—for example, speaking in front of a group of people we don't know—that old mechanism kicks in and our body gets prepared for fight or flight. Modern, civilized life doesn't leave us much room for fighting.

As a result, we have nowhere to turn to relieve this stress. Our ancestors burned away their stress by defending themselves or hightailing it out of town. But we have to bottle it up and stand there. That internalized energy causes all those unpleasant physical sensations we call nerves, platform jitters, the shakes, and so on.

Fear: A distressing emotion aroused by an impending pain, danger, or evil; or by the illusion of such.

Step 4: Learn to Work with Your Body's Physical Reaction

Positive thinking won't make the symptoms of nervousness disappear altogether, but it will greatly reduce your body's tendency to get nervous. Sometimes, as I mentioned, your body can be treacherous. Even though you know better, even though you think positively, your body insists on "feeling" nervous. Unfortunately, the appearance of nervousness is often more than enough to trigger the reality of nervousness.

The good news is that once you know a handful of "secret" techniques, dealing with nervousness will be far easier. The key to gaining control of your body's reaction to the fight-or-flight instinct is to understand that the symptoms of nervousness come from the tension of not being able to burn off the fight-or-flight adrenaline. Burn off the excess energy, relax, and you will reduce the feeling of nervousness.

To reduce physical stress, try the following:

➤ **Deep breathing**. This helps control stress by returning your breathing to its natural, pre-stress patterns. Try taking a few deep breaths, then attempt to breathe normally.

➤ **Isometric exercises**. These are stationary exercises in which one group of muscles works against another. Try pressing your fingertips gently together, then press harder and hold for a few seconds. You can do these as you begin speaking—no one will know that you're burning bottled stress and reducing nervousness.

Secrets of the Pros

"If you are nervous, that's normal. Remember, we were all nervous the first time we got on a bicycle."
—Tony Walker

➤ **Vigorous exercises**. These are activities such as jogging, walking, or swimming. A night or two before your presentation, take time out to go for a walk. If you're still nervous just before your presentation, find a storage room or empty restroom and do a few vigorous jumping jacks. Don't drench yourself in sweat, just do enough to get the blood flowing. It's a great stress reducer.

Nervous to Natural

➤ **Relaxation techniques.** These should focus on tense muscle groups. First relax your scalp, then your eyebrows and ears, then your tongue and jaw, then shoulders and on down to your feet. Repeat as necessary, or try stretching in combination with this technique.

➤ **Yawning.** This is the body's natural way of relaxing itself. It also stretches the muscles of your neck to allow more natural speaking. Try yawning widely a few times.

➤ **Talking to yourself.** This is different from self-talking. Here I *literally* mean talk to yourself to warm up your voice. One trick is to practice saying "Good morning!" over and over as you're on your way to a presentation. People may look at you as if you're nuts, but it's a small price to pay to reduce nervousness and prepare yourself for a great presentation!

➤ **Move and gesture.** As you begin to speak, move and gesture in order to burn off nervous energy. It catches your audience's attention when you're animated.

➤ **Pausing.** This conveys relaxation and confidence. Once you begin to speak, nerves can make you speak quickly, alerting everyone to your nervous state. This can be controlled by learning to pause. Surprisingly, a pause of two or three seconds not only catches the attention of the audience but also lets them know you're in command. Learn to use the power of silence!

Practice one or more of these techniques regularly and tailor them to your own particular patterns of nervousness. Combined with positive *self-talk,* they represent a powerful combination for combating nervousness.

Step 5: Bonding with the Audience

Don't be too concerned if a touch of nervous energy remains as you approach the front of the room. It's useful energy at this point. In fact, it's something you can use to build excitement, project

Secrets of the Pros

"Get there early and meet some people up close, and use their names."
—Patrick O'Dooley, C.S.P.

enthusiasm, and create a bond with the audience. Building an early rapport helps boost your confidence and increases the audience's natural urge to want you to succeed.

Bonding with your audience begins long before you start to speak.

➤ **Arrive early.** By arriving before your audience members, you send the message that you care enough to get things ready in advance.

➤ **Meet and greet the audience yourself.** I never cease to be amazed by presenters who stand off in one corner or officiously read notes while their audience files in. Get on your feet and greet! This is a great opportunity to build rapport. Always ask for their names, shake their hands, and make solid eye contact. When time allows, ask how far they drove to get to the presentation, where they work, and other personal information. This provides you with important material and begins the process of developing audience advocates.

➤ **Start by grabbing your audience's attention.** Get your audience involved immediately! This will encourage them to *buy-in* to what you say for the rest of your presentation (See chapter 4, "The First Three Minutes," for details).

➤ **Let your audience know what's in it for them.** Begin with a statement that reduces their nervousness. (Yes, your audience is nervous—everyone is!) Let them know they aren't wasting their time.

Reducing Nervousness

Your audience is almost as nervous as you are. Involve them as soon as possible to calm everyone's nerves. One icebreaker you might try is to have everyone share his or her favorite hobby, quote, or a bit of background information about themselves. This is usually a winner that lets people have fun and helps get your butterflies flying in formation.

Nervous to Natural

➤ **Make eye contact**. Search out a few friendly faces—those folks who are smiling, nodding at what you say, laughing at your jokes. Draw power by making eye contact. A good place to start is with those few brave souls seated in the front.

➤ **Show genuine enthusiasm**. Let your audience know you're happy to be there, and they will be too. This will help to reduce your nervousness and make you more comfortable.

You probably didn't know all or even most of this information beforehand. Learning these things can help you make friends with your audience. Getting that information beforehand greatly increases your success rate and confidence, thereby reducing or even eliminating your nervousness.

You might have heard how important it is to "build a rapport" with your audience—that is, getting them to know and like you. But has anyone ever told you that building a rapport begins before you ever see them? The research you do even a day or two before you meet your audience can make a big difference. They will begin to know and like you at the beginning of the talk if you have begun to know (and like) them before the talk.

One More Note on Nerves

Nervousness doesn't have to be your enemy. It's a natural, healthy sign. The day I stop feeling nervous is the day I know I'm no longer an effective presenter. Make your nervousness work for

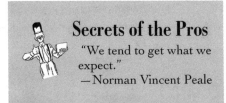

Secrets of the Pros

"We tend to get what we expect."
—Norman Vincent Peale

you rather than against you. Always strive to appear poised. It's one of the few miracles of the real world. The more you practice not *looking* nervous, the more your nervousness subsides. And finally, never apologize to your audience for feeling nervous. Your audience has no idea you're feeling the jitters. Only you can let them know, so don't!

Bond with Your Audience

When you stand up to talk to your children (or friends or relatives), do you feel nervous? In most situations, probably not. Why? Because you know them. What makes other audiences scary is that we simply have too little information about them.

Think of the last group to which you spoke. Did you know:

➤ **What your audience members' names were?**

➤ **Why they were in the room with you?**

➤ **What they expected to get from listening to you?**

➤ **What was in your talk for them?**

➤ **What their likes and dislikes were?**

➤ **What level of knowledge they brought to your discussion?**

➤ **How to pronounce their names individually?**

➤ **What kinds of presentation have worked for this group or one like it in the past?**

➤ **What kind of jokes they liked?**

Very Important Points To Remember

✔ Everyone gets nervous—it's a natural physical reaction that can be controlled, both mentally and physically.

✔ Your audience *wants* you to win.

✔ Being completely prepared is the key to reducing nervousness.

✔ Use positive *self-talk* to reduce your mental stress.

✔ Use appropriate stress and tension reduction exercises to lessen your physical stress.

✔ Convert nervousness to enthusiasm by bonding with your audience. Get them involved immediately.

✔ Practice feeling confident and you will be confident. Never let 'em see you sweat!

Fill in Your Favorite Tips from the Chapter

✔ _____
_____

✔ _____
_____

✔ _____
_____

✔ _____
_____

✔ _____
_____

✔ _____
_____

✔ _____
_____

✔ _____
_____

✔ _____
_____

✔ _____
_____

✔ _____
_____

✔ _____
_____

✔ _____
_____

✔ _____
_____

PART 2
Beginning Your Presentation

This chapter reveals:

➤ How to get off to a great start by building rapport and earning respect

➤ A collection of audience-grabbing openers

➤ The four "audience-tensions" and how to alleviate them

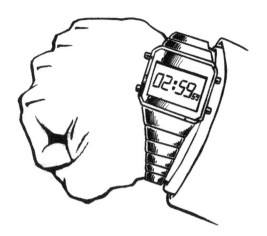

4

The First
Three Minutes

"You are an unknown quantity for only 120 seconds. After that everything you say will be heard in the context of the impression from your first two minutes."

— David Peoples
Presentations Plus

The Scene ...

This is it! You've prepared, you've rehearsed, you've brought your nervousness under control, and now you're ready for the big time! You're delivering a presentation at the annual convention to a group of 150 knowledgeable professionals from around the country.

You've been at the front of the room before, and you know that beginning a presentation is a little like piloting an airplane — takeoff is the most critical phase. If they don't *buy-in* now, you'll be playing catch-up all week. What you need is a surefire system for the first three minutes to grab the audience's attention, build rapport, and ensure that they will buy in immediately to what you're saying.

The Solution . . .

Know the secrets of creating a great first three minutes.

The first *three* minutes are different from the rest of your presentation for the following reasons:

➤ **Your audience's attention is naturally high.**

➤ **Most audiences spend the first 180 seconds of any presentation sizing up the presenter.**

➤ **You have only one chance to make a first impression.**

➤ **First impressions are lasting impressions and are, therefore, a speaker's best opportunity to win an audience.**

Secrets

1. **Show respect and build rapport.**
   ➤ **Make the audience your partner.**
   ➤ **Prove you respect their time.**
   ➤ **Prove you're prepared.**
   ➤ **Empathize with your audience and communicate similar interests.** (Show commonality — people like people who are like themselves.)
   ➤ **Use eye contact** — it's an attention-grabber.

2. **Grab the audience's attention and run with it.**
   ➤ **Find a hook.**
   ➤ **Use an attention-grabber (an immediate benefit or concurrence for/from the audience).**
   ➤ **Know and use the different types of openers:**
      • **Current event**
      • **Humorous**
      • **Pictorial**
      • **Anecdotal**
      • **Pertinent quote**

- Real-world situation
- Rhetorical
- Musical

➤ *Four* sure ways to *kill* an opening are the following:
- An apology
- An unrelated or inappropriate anecdote
- Long- or slow-moving statements
- Equipment failure

➤ "Must-Dos" in the first *three* minutes:
- Focus wandering minds on the topic at hand.
- Use appropriate words and gestures.
- Get your audience committed to staying involved.

Step 1: Show Respect and Build Rapport

In the preceding chapter, we discussed the fact that most audiences want the speaker to succeed. Even a negative audience has a vested interest in your success. The more successful you are, the more enjoyable your presentation will be, even for them. There are *three* things every audience loves:

1. **Respect** (for their time, their dignity, their feelings, etc.)

2. **Rapport** (between themselves and the speaker)

3. **Entertainment**

These *three* elements provide a threshold for audience buy-in, involvement, and satisfaction. The first words out of your mouth should carry your audience over this threshold and prove that you will, above all else, deliver these three audience imperatives.

Why the First Three Minutes?

In the first three minutes of your presentation, your audience is sizing you up. They're deciding whether they like you and you like them. They're also wondering whether or not you're worth listening to. Grab them early, and they'll stick by you even if something goes wrong later; however, if you lose them, you will be playing catch-up for the rest of your presentation.

The First Three Minutes

Make the Audience Your Partner

The way to guarantee an audience's commitment and loyalty to you is to immediately involve them in your presentation! There's an old saying, "Nobody believes they have an ugly baby." So the key to audience buy-in (a prerequisite for audience inspiration) is to make them part-owner of the presentation—make the presentation half *their* baby! Once your audience has taken partial ownership of the presentation, you are destined for success, because your audience will not let you fail. There are *three* steps to making the audience your partner:

> ### Secrets of the Pros
>
> "I first try to get them to move forward. Then I remind myself that the ones who did show up deserve the best that I've got and I try to give it to them."
>
> —Jeff Slutsky
> Streetfighter Marketing

1. **Meet as many attendees as possible *before* the presentation.** This begins to build a one-on-one bond that will carry over into the first few minutes of your presentation.

2. **Prove you respect them by starting the presentation on time.**

3. **Ask them to define their own expectations.**

Step three deserves special attention. Asking the audience to define their own expectations gives them a feeling of input and control and lets them know you care about their feelings. You can write their expectations on a flip chart, let them know which expectations you can reasonably meet and which ones you cannot, and then use that page again later to prove you've delivered value.

Prove That You Respect Their Time

You've put a lot of effort into preparing your presentation: hours, days, maybe weeks. Why? Because you care about your audience and respect their time. Unfortunately, audiences have no way of knowing this *unless you tell them.* An audience expects the room to be set up, the speaker to be well-prepared and well-groomed, and all manner of things to be in order when they arrive—so it doesn't always occur to them how much time and preparation went into getting ready.

At some point in your first three minutes, let them know that because you respect their time, hours and hours of preparation have been invested in your presentation. Let audience members know that your respect for their valuable time will continue throughout the presentation.

Prove That You're Prepared

Nothing sends the message that you don't care like being unprepared. Every detail counts—starting on time, having the appropriate materials ready, knowing what you're going to say. The audience notices everything. If they get the feeling that you are ill-prepared, they'll tune you out. In order to better demonstrate preparedness, make sure you're prepared with the answers to some questions that will be important to them. Such questions might include:

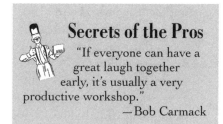

Secrets of the Pros

"If everyone can have a great laugh together early, it's usually a very productive workshop."
—Bob Carmack

➤ **Who are you?**

➤ **How long is the day scheduled to run?**

➤ **How frequently will breaks be taken?**

➤ **What can be gained from the presentation?**

➤ **Where are the restrooms, telephones, and smoking areas located?**

First Impressions

Audiences gain their first impressions of a speaker from *four* areas:

➤ **Appearance**—dress and grooming
➤ **Orderliness**—room setup, materials
➤ **Qualities as a host**—making audiences comfortable
➤ **Credibility**—knowledge of subject and speaking ability

—Doug Kevorkian

Use Eye Contact

Nothing builds rapport faster than eye contact. Think of all the clichés you've heard. You don't believe a word from the "shifty-eyed salesman"; you can't trust someone who's afraid to "look you in the eye"; the eyes are the "windows to the soul"; and you "eye something suspiciously" if you don't trust it.

Start your first three minutes by making solid eye contact with a few members of the audience. Don't scan the audience — speak *to* individual audience members and make eye contact while doing so. Even those members of the audience with whom you're not making eye contact will benefit because they will be able to see that you *are* talking to individuals. In addition to creating the impression that you are confident and honest, eye contact keeps your audience alert and communicates your interest in them.

> **Secrets of the Pros**
>
> "I always strive to get the audience into the subject as quickly as possible. Many times, my first statement is a question looking for a response. This is a tremendous icebreaker."
> — Paul Boitmann

The Twelve Commandments

Building rapport is critical for achieving audience buy-in — and without 100 percent buy-in, it's terribly difficult to inspire an audience to act. In fact, audience rapport is so important that I've coined the following **Twelve Commandments of Building and Maintaining Rapport:**

1. **Thou shalt respect thy audience.**

2. **Whenever possible, thou shalt meet with members of thy audience *before* thy talk.** Shake their hands, ask their names, and begin to know them as individuals. This will create an early bond that should last throughout the talk.

3. **Thou shalt start on time.**

4. **When possible, thou shalt bestow small presents upon thy audience members.**

5. Thou shalt maintain good eye contact with individuals, avoiding the temptation to scan thy audience.

6. Thou shalt attempt to learn and use some of thy audience's own buzz words, acronyms, and jargon whenever possible and, of course, acknowledge audience members by name.

> **Eye Contact**
>
> The eyes don't lie. If the first words out of your mouth are, "I'm thrilled to be here," but you're staring at the floor in front of your feet, your audience will learn not to trust a word you say. That's definitely *not* a favorable first impression.

7. Thou shalt convey appreciation—nothing connects two people better than a sincere compliment.

8. Thou shalt use breaks to continue nurturing rapport; socialize with thy audience!

9. Thou shalt seek feedback, especially on issues that affect audience comfort such as: room temperature, volume level, speed of thy talk, etc.

10. Thou shalt praise audience members and make them heroes.

11. Thou shalt learn to be a good listener: give good eye contact, pause, listen to the entire statement, and nary make a joke about an audience member's comment.

12. **Thou shalt mirror thy audience's speaking patterns.** If they talk fast, talk fast; if they speak slowly, slow down.

Step 2. Grab the Audience's Attention

Finding a Hook

How many times have you heard a speaker start with this line: "Good morning (afternoon, evening), ladies and gentlemen"? Dozens? Hundreds? It's the tiredest line in any speaker's repertoire, yet speakers and presenters return to it time and again. It's comfortable, expected, and BORING!

Rather than starting off with a line no one hears—it's the speaking equivalent of asking, "How are you?"—try to open with a line that

89

grabs the audience's attention and makes them listen. The line doesn't have to be outrageous, just interesting. It should also be something that gets the audience involved at some level, even if it is only to raise their hands or answer a question.

> **Secrets of the Pros**
>
> "Remember to show the audience that you are human. Let them know that you have the same desires, challenges and stresses that they have. This may be your greatest source of credibility."
> —Sherry Boecher

Here are a few surefire ways to make your audience listen:

➤ **Begin with a startling statistic.** "Nearly everyone in this room has passed up an opportunity to become a millionaire."

➤ **Begin with a proactive question.** "How many of you in this room have purchased a foreign-made product this week?"

➤ **Tell a story about something that recently happened to you.**

➤ **Refer to some current newsworthy event.** Make sure it applies to the subject at hand.

Use hooks to signal that you're different from some of the other presenters your audience may have seen, many of whom began their presentations with clunkers like these:

➤ **Good morning, ladies and gentlemen.**

➤ **Let's review some administrative details.**

➤ **I'm not much of a speaker, but here goes . . . .**

Consider the following when searching for openers that grab an audience's attention and get them involved.

Know Your Openers!

Current Event. People are interested in current events. Open with a comment on some local or national event that will get them interested. Especially effective are current events relating to human interest, new findings, car and home prices. Avoid politics, religion, and other controversial topics.

Humor. Start with a funny story, observation, or activity. Make sure it is pertinent to the topic at hand or illustrates some point you wish the audience to understand. Laughing gets the audience on your side! As a rule, avoid jokes. They sound canned, usually have nothing to do with the topic, and always seem to offend someone.

An anecdote. Share an anecdote that illustrates some important concept included in your presentation. The key to using anecdotes is to keep them short and to the point. It's better to tell a short story and leave the audience wanting more than to draw a story out and bore them.

A quotation. Quotations are often filled with wisdom, and carry authority. They can sometimes make a point more clearly than we can. Use them. Books packed with good quotes from different people on hundreds of subjects can be found in the reference section of any library or bookstore.

A real-world situation. A recognizable scene grabs attention. Audiences respond to "seeing themselves" in a situation. (See the beginning of each chapter in this book.)

A question. Questions are great because they require an answer. Ask something provocative and a little mysterious about the audience, such as, "How many of you have a remote-control television at home?" Then tie the question to a point you wish to make.

Trivia, statistics, little-known facts. Did you know that a person's heart pumps one million times in an average lifetime? That the average lightning bolt has enough energy to light up a city? That more Americans are injured in auto accidents each year than were injured in all of our wars combined? Neither does your audience. Using appropriate facts and trivia affects your audience like a jolt of adrenaline.

Music. Music is powerful stuff—it will awaken the audience, and it can also be used to make a point. Go for high-energy, upbeat music when you want to crank up audience energy.

Freebies. People love free stuff, so give something away. Even the smallest trinkets can serve as a memento for your presentation.

Probably my biggest trademark as a presenter is giving away dollar bills. I have a pad of brand-new, mint dollar bills put on a cardboard backing with a gummy spine. I give them to audience members during the first three minutes to get the room laughing and warmed up—then throughout the day to reward funny comments, special help, and so on. It's always a hit and well worth the few dollars it costs me.

Five Sure Ways to Kill Your Opening

There are plenty of good ways to open your presentation effectively. And there are *five* sure ways to ruin your opening. Whatever else you do in your first three minutes, remember the following:

1. **Never start late**. This sends the signal that everything you say is subject to change. Pick a starting time and stick with it.

2. **Never start with an apology**. Don't apologize for anything. If it's a big mistake, your audience will see it and, believe me, they'll know you're sorry. If it's a small mistake, they won't notice it unless you bring it to their attention by apologizing. And never start a story or comical anecdote with an apologetic disclaimer like, "I'm not much of a comedian, but here goes . . . ." Doing so sets you up for failure. Always think positively.

3. **Never start with an unrelated or inappropriate anecdote**. A presentation has to be *about* something. If your stories or anecdotes are unrelated to the topic, they will confuse your audience. Never use a racy anecdote in front of an audience. The dividends from a good anecdote and a laugh are great but never great enough to risk alienating even a few of your audience members with an offensive remark.

4. **Never start slowly**. Open with a bang and *move*. Always stay a step ahead of the audience. This doesn't mean talk fast; it means don't dawdle when telling stories or making points. Avoid opening with boring material such as administrative matters. Save that sort of thing for the middle section of your speech and, even then, keep it brief.

> ### Secrets of the Pros
>
> "Words have power. Words have altered the course of history and changed forever the destiny of individuals who spoke out."
> —Terrence J. McCann
> Executive Director
> Toastmasters International

Quotations

Quotations are great for a number of reasons. They have built-in brevity—part of what makes a quotation work is that it is short and to-the-point. Quotations usually contain an element of essential truth, the I-know-exactly-what-you-mean quality that delights readers and listeners. Many have withstood the test of time, dating back thousands of years.

When using quotations, follow these simple rules.

1. **Make sure the quote reinforces your message.**

2. **Include some background information to make the quote meaningful.** Henry Ford will require a little less background than Thucydides.

3. **Make sure it is related; avoid being a showoff.** Too many quotes or quotes from obscure sources may give the impression that you *think* you know a lot. It's ok to be smart, but rubbing your audience's face in your knowledge is the surest way to turn them off.

4. **Quote correctly.** Misquoting can kill your credibility, especially if someone in your audience points it out. Always write out any quotation you're using word for word. When in doubt, paraphrase. Make sure you pronounce the name of your source correctly.

5. **Never start with equipment failure**. No matter how well you've prepared, if your microphone fails, your VCR monitor isn't ready, or the light bulb on your overhead projector is burned out, you'll look ill-prepared. If something breaks while you're using it, *never* stop to repair it. Acknowledge the problem, then move on. Audiences understand that accidents happen; what they don't understand is having to wait for you to fix something. It's better to skip something than make your audience wait for a troubleshooter to come in and fix a broken piece of equipment!

Make Sure Your Body Reinforces What You Say

A few years ago, some researchers at UCLA conducted a study that has become famous in the presentation world. In it they found

laugh at my jokes, I hope." I also maintain early eye contact with them to draw power from their interest and attention.

➤ **Create a conversational tone.** People love having a conversation, but they do not like being lectured to. Avoid the tone of a lecture. Ask questions, seek audience opinion, and use plain language and short declarative sentences. (See chapter 6 for more on "Setting the Tone" and having a conversation with your audience.)

> **Secrets of the Pros**
>
> "Even if you keep on giving the same speech over and over again (remember that technique helped make Ronald Reagan president of the United States), always find out the names of some people in the audience and what they especially came for. When you get to that point in your presentation, look across the room and say, 'Tom you'll be especially interested in this point.'"
>
> —Dr. Jeffrey Lant

➤ **Move among your audience.** If the size of the group allows, walk into the audience as you speak. Whenever possible, avoid podiums.

Know How to Gesture Effectively

Gestures are important, especially in your first three minutes. They create a dynamic atmosphere, hold the audience's attention, and communicate what kind of speaker you are. Yet despite their importance, many speakers, even accomplished ones, take gestures for granted. It's worth the time to study and practice the how-tos of effective gesturing.

Gestures can be grouped into *three* major categories:

1. **Descriptive gestures.** These are used to clarify or enhance a verbal message. They help the audience understand comparisons and contrasts and visualize the size, shape, movement, location, function, and number of objects.

2. **Suggestive gestures.** These are symbols of ideas and emotions. They help a speaker create a desired mood or express a particular thought.

3. **Prompting gestures.** These are used to help evoke a desired response from the audience.

Gestures are reflective of each speaker's individual personality. What's right for one speaker might not work for you. If you suspect that your presence is not dynamic enough, learn to use gestures appropriately by following these simple guidelines:

➤ **Respond naturally.**

➤ **Suit the gesture to the words.**

➤ **Make your gestures convincing.**

➤ **Make your gestures smooth and well-timed.**

The following is a list of common gestures and how audiences tend to perceive them:

➤ **Pointing.** Pointing your index finger can emphasize a statement or call attention to an idea, but it can also be taken as an accusation. Use it sparingly

➤ **Palms down.** Both palms down indicates weight or decisiveness. A sweeping gesture with one arm, palm down, dismisses something, as in, "We won't even talk about that."

➤ **Palms up.** Both arms, palms up invites a group to stand. It is also a gesture used to ask for something. It can be taken as an offer when you're giving out something like an idea worth thinking about.

➤ **Chopping.** A chopping motion with one hand shows where something ends and something else begins. It can also be used to make a point. It's not as strong as pointing but stronger than no gesture at all.

➤ **Palm out.** Like a signal to halt used by a traffic cop, this gesture slows an audience down. It can be used to move from laughter to seriousness or to introduce a new idea.

➤ **Raised fist.** A raised fist shows determination or anger. It is also, of course, a signal for fighting. Be careful with this one!

STEP 3. Know the Four Audience Tensions and Work to Alleviate Them

It's not a widely known fact, but every audience, however large or small, has *four* natural and usually subconscious tensions. Become acquainted with these tensions and begin dealing with them *immediately*.

Four tensions exist between:

1. **The audience and the audience.** Members of the audience usually don't know each other well. This causes apprehension.

2. **The audience and the presenter. Because audience members usually don't know the presenter well,** they feel some natural tension toward the presenter and the presenter has similar feelings toward the audience.

3. **The audience and their materials.** Audience members are often given notepads, pens, pencils, notebooks, and other materials.

> **Secrets of the Pros**
>
> "Always start your speech off by thanking particular people from the host organization. Be just as effusive about them as you can be. Remember, not least, they're writing your testimonials!"
> —Dr. Jeffrey Lant

4. **The audience and their environment.** An unfamiliar environment is sure to cause tension, but even when audience members know the room, the speaker and the equipment used will produce tension.

Just being aware that these *four* tensions exist will make you a better presenter. Far too few presenters ever give them any thought. It's a shame, since alleviating these tensions is really a matter of following a few simple, common-sense steps:

Audience and Audience

➤ **Get the audience up and moving.**

➤ **Get the audience to shake hands and socialize with one another.**

Audience and Instructor

➤ **Build audience rapport.**

➤ **Establish and maintain eye contact.**

➤ **Smile.**

Audience and Materials

➤ **Involve the audience with their materials immediately.** Don't leave handouts and notebooks in front of them unexplained.

➤ **Instruct the audience to *immediately* write their names on their materials.** This will begin the "ownership process" and reduce tension.

➤ **Hand out materials only when participants need them.** This reduces tension and keeps the audience from being distracted by their materials.

Audience and Environment

➤ **Be aware of the environment.**

➤ **Try to make it as comfortable as possible.**

➤ **Seek and act on feedback concerning comfort issues such as seating, room temperature, lighting, sound volume, etc.**

Secrets of the Pros

"Consider a one-page handout for short presentations."

— Dale Ware

➤ **If some comfort issue is beyond your control (hard chairs, poor ventilation), add breaks to your agenda.** It's better to have a few extra breaks than an uncomfortable audience squirming in their seats.

Very Important Points To Remember

✔ You have about three minutes to win an audience. Make the most of them!

✔ Build rapport by hooking your audience, proving you value their time, and letting them know where you're headed.

✔ Research shows that 7 percent of a presentation's outcome is contingent upon words, 38 percent on tonality and 55 percent on body language. Maximize the 93 percent that isn't words. It isn't what you say but how you say it!

✔ Know the tensions that every audience member feels and work to ease those tensions during your opening.

Fill in Your Favorite Tips from the Chapter

✔ _____

_____

✔ _____

_____

The First Three Minutes

99

This chapter reveals:

➤ What credibility means

➤ Tips for proving to your audience that you have the right to be at the front of the room

➤ How to build credibility with any audience in minutes

5

Being Credible

JEARY THEORY

Credibility flows from you to the audience. You must
tell the truth and be real to earn true credibility.

"To win, we must be believed. To be believed, we
must be believable. To be believable, we must tell the
truth. . . ."

— Gerry Spence

The Scene . . .

You know your subject and you're well prepared for your first big
presentation out of school, but you've got one problem — your
resumé. How can you let your audience know how much you know
when you've only recently graduated from college? Many of your
colleagues (and even some of your audience members) have
impressive credentials; how can you convince them that you know
what you're talking about?

The Solution . . .

Always keep in mind that the audience's impression of you is the
single most important factor when establishing your credibility.

That's why it is so important to build rapport and show respect for your audience in the first three minutes of your presentation. A positive rapport lays the foundation for your audience and establishes your honesty. Many experts fail as presenters because they rub the audience the wrong way. Understand the power of establishing your credibility!

Secrets

1. **Know what real credibility is.**

   ➤ **Know that you will be judged on the following:**

   - **Depth of knowledge**
   - **Personal experiences**
   - **Level of preparedness**
   - **Enthusiasm during the presentation**
   - **Appearance**
   - **Language (body and verbal)**

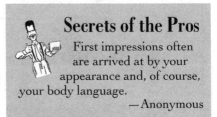

Secrets of the Pros

First impressions often are arrived at by your appearance and, of course, your body language.

—Anonymous

   ➤ **Is credibility an illusion or reality?**

2. **Tell the truth.**

   ➤ **Commit and adhere to a time requirement up front.**

   ➤ **Make a note when you say you will do something, then do it!**

3. **Explain why you have the right to talk to them.**

   ➤ **The more relevant the introduction, the higher your credibility.**

   ➤ **Share personal experiences with your audience.**

4. **Connect with the audience.**

   ➤ **Be natural**

   ➤ **Be sincere**

   ➤ **Be enthusiastic**

   ➤ **Be spontaneous**

What Is Credibility?

Ever wonder why banks look the way they do? I'm not necessarily talking about the local branch at the corner, but rather the big international banks, the Federal Reserve in Washington, D.C., or the huge investment houses on Wall Street. Walking into these banks is a breathtaking experience. Soaring ceilings, vaulted arches, marble floors. In fact, only two other types of architectural structures come close to the inspiring drama of a large bank: castles and cathedrals.

Why? Because these buildings are large, awe-inspiring, eternal-looking structures that *inspire* credibility. This brings us to the essential paradox of credibility. On the one hand, it is very real—what could be more real than the rule of kings, the influence of priests, or the power of bankers? On the other hand, credibility is often subjective and always just an illusion. No one except God is truly permanent or utterly trustworthy.

> **Secrets of the Pros**
>
> "One of the things I like to do, whenever possible, is to go around the room and have everyone personally introduce themselves to ME. I'll write down their names and seating positions. This helps me get to know and remember them. Throughout the workshop, I'll always refer to them by name—it makes them feel important and that the training is more personal."
> —Bob Carmack

The bottom line is this: Credibility is something that is *bestowed* upon one person by one or more other people. It might be the result of hard work; but, hard work in and of itself does not build credibility (sad but true). Unless people give you *credit* for the work you do, you can never gain credibility. The trick for you as a presenter is to demonstrate the *qualities* that make people want to bestow credibility upon you.

Qualities that instill credibility include:

1. **Integrity.** Be yourself.

2. **Expertise.**

> **Secrets of the Pros**
>
> "Let the crowd know you've been there.'"
> —Steve Richards

3. Empathy.

4. Awareness of your own power.

In the next few sections, we will explore these qualities and provide techniques for demonstrating them to your audience.

Integrity/Be Yourself

Are you honest enough for the audience to believe you? Audiences can see through pretension immediately, and it doesn't take them much longer to see through any of the other forms of dishonesty. You can be sure the audience gets a sense of your integrity by doing the following:

➤ **Telling the truth.** Your audience will never really trust you if they catch you in a lie.

➤ **Being yourself.** Trying to be someone you're not is almost as bad as telling a lie. It's also a lot more work.

➤ **Doing what you say you will.** If you say you're starting at 8:30 a.m., then start at 8:30 a.m. If you promise frequent breaks, allow for frequent breaks.

➤ **Speak with conviction.** Say it like you mean it, and your audience will believe in your words.

➤ **Never pretend to know the answer to a question and *never* fake it.** It's better to say "I don't know" and try to help the audience find the answer.

People Want You To Be Honest and Want To Hear What You Have To Say

W. P. "Buz" Barlow Jr., a prominent Dallas attorney, took time from his busy practice to serve as Special Counsel to Dr. Robert Schuller. While based at the Crystal Cathedral in Southern California, Buz contributed to *The Hour of Power* television program seen weekly all over the world and spoke to audiences in more than 50 cities across the United

> **Secrets of the Pros**
>
> "Never speak after an animal act or a cute kid. They have tricks you just can't use anymore and retain any credibility at all."
>
> —Dr. Jeffrey Lant

States. Upon his return home, he was asked to take the pulpit of the prestigious, 8,000-member Lovers Lane United Methodist Church to preach all three Sunday morning services. He relates the following story:

> Having had my own radio show, having done a national television commercial with Steve Allen, and having been a trial lawyer for more than 25 years, I've grown accustomed to "performing" under just about any circumstances. I nevertheless found the prospect of bearing my soul to the members of my church family under the watchful eye of my dear friend and mentor, Dr. Don Benton, a formidable task.
>
> I prayed that I would be worthy of the sacred trust given to me, and I prepared as never before to find just the right blend of anecdotes, scriptural references, and positive thinking. Don had taught the preaching course at Southern Methodist University's Perkins School of Theology, and it was his long-held belief that a message should be scripted, practiced from text, and then delivered without the benefit of notes. I knew I'd let him down if I deviated from this time-tested formula, and I had no intention of doing that.
>
> After countless rewrites, my draft finally completed, I was ready for Dr. Benton to give his blessing to the content and to receive any last-minute advice he deemed appropriate. He sent me off with words of encouragement and some wise counsel I'll never forget because it applied to every speaking situation imaginable. "Buz," he began, "people want to hear what you have to say and you're obviously well prepared, so now just go out and preach it!"

"Just preach it" means to give of yourself, to share what is within you rather than to recite memorized lines or worse yet, to

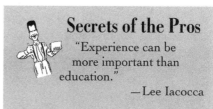

Secrets of the Pros

"Experience can be more important than education."

—Lee Iacocca

merely read from note cards. Without passion and conviction, communication at any level suffers. We can't expect anyone to listen if we don't act like what we're saying is important and meaningful to them.

So always remember to prepare, to practice, and to preach it.

Expertise

As renowned speaker Anthony Robbins suggests, "You don't have to know everything to use everything!" In other words, you don't have to be an expert to have expertise. Experts are people who have spent their whole lives learning about a certain subject. Though I have known many

Secrets of the Pros

"A great way to find out whether you are being authentic or not is to practice in front of teenagers. If you hear, 'You don't sound like yourself, Mom'—even once— you've been given a valuable piece of input."

—Judy Chaffee

experts who can speak wonderfully, I've also met some real duds. An expert can often get hung up on forcing an audience to see things the way he or she sees it. This alienates an audience and makes the expert seem less credible. When an audience doesn't like a speaker, they won't give him credit for the expertise he spent so much time acquiring.

It's easier for a good speaker to pick up a basic level of expertise than for a subject matter expert to become a great speaker. Follow these steps to increase your expertise on any subject:

➤ **Know your subject.** Carefully prepare what you will and won't say.

➤ **Do your homework.** Request manuals, workbooks, textbooks, training videos, and any other materials that can bring you up to speed when dealing with an unfamiliar subject.

➤ **Use the audience's language.** Learn and use some of the terms your audience knows. This will demonstrate that you took time to prepare.

Enthusiasm

If you are glad to be in front of the room, most audiences will be glad to have you there. Enthusiasm sends the signal that you, the speaker, are comfortable and in control of the situation. The audience will believe in you if you have the confidence and energy to be enthusiastic about your own presentation.

Remember the following:

➤ **Appeal to emotion.** People are persuaded more by emotion than by logic. The expert sometimes makes the mistake of thinking only logic matters. Combine logic with *emotional* persuasion.

➤ **Work the *entire* room.** Don't fall into the trap of speaking to just one or two people. Speak to everyone in the room. Make eye contact with as many audience members as possible. Don't pick favorites!

Empathy

Convince your audience that you understand how things look from their perspective. Prove it by letting them know you are there for them and not for yourself.

Remember the following:

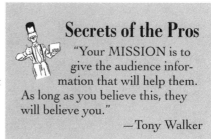

Secrets of the Pros

"Your MISSION is to give the audience information that will help them. As long as you believe this, they will believe you."

—Tony Walker

➤ **People like people who seem familiar.** Identify with your audience and prove that you are one of them. This doesn't mean you should mimic or patronize them, only that you should strive to see things from their point of view.

➤ **Identify with someone the audience admires.** Remember back in chapter 1, when you developed a list of people your audience was likely to admire? Let the audience know that you know the people they know. This will help them transfer to you the natural trust they feel for people they admire.

➤ **Let your audience know that you understand.** Listening is hard work. Take breaks, listen to concerns, and seek feedback from your audience members.

➤ **Dress like your audience dresses.** This helps you look and feel like one of them.

Awareness of Your Own Power

Believable people know they are believable—and they exude this awareness. You have to convince yourself of your own credibility before you can convince the audience.

Try these suggestions:

➤ **Share personal experiences.** This provides an opportunity for the audience to relate to you.

➤ **Introduce yourself.** Let them know why you are speaking to them.

> **How Your Audience Will Judge You**
> ✓ Depth of knowledge
> ✓ Personal experiences
> ✓ Level of preparedness
> ✓ Enthusiasm
> ✓ Appearance
> ✓ Body language

Let me share a couple of experiences with you. I went to Zig Ziglar's home after watching him make numerous presentations to thousands of people. I was impressed with how real and how humble Zig is, both in front of a room and behind the scenes.

You must be real to be credible. As Gerry Spence states in his great book, *How to Argue and Win Every Time*, people have "imaginary credibility feelers" that sense your realness.

Another good example of this principle is Dr. Ken Blanchard. I had the opportunity a few years back to meet with him for an hour or so after a chance encounter in the airport in Dallas. I had

> **Secrets of the Pros**
> "Winston Churchill once said, 'What the people really want to hear is the truth. It is an exciting thing to speak the truth.'"
> —Gerry Spence

listened to him, read his works, and admired him for many years. To see that he is the same one-on-one as he is in front of groups was a memorable experience for me.

Conduct yourself in the same manner in front of an audience as you would in front of a friend. Be yourself.

One group of people that understands how important it is to create a perception of credibility in an audience is lawyers. The following are selections from attorney Gerry Spence's terrific book, *How to Argue and Win Every Time:*

> One can stand as the greatest orator the world has known, possess the quickest mind, employ the cleverest psychology, and have mastered all the technical devices of argument, but if one is not credible, one might just as well preach to the pelicans.

> While the lie detector with its operator may take minutes, even hours to complete its analysis of a single sentence, our minds, as rapidly as the words fall from the speaker's mouth, record split-second conclusions concerning the speaker's credibility.

Tell Them Why You Have the Right To Be in Front of Them

It might be hard for you to believe, but you have the right to be in front of the room. Unfortunately, it is not enough to know this. You must come right out and *tell* the audience why you have the right to be in front of them. Mention the following:

➤ **Your personal experiences**

➤ **Your knowledge and skill as a presenter**

➤ **Your credentials**

> **Secrets of the Pros**
>
> "Who is in fact the smartest, most important person in the room? It certainly is not you. After all, the people in the room don't perceive a need for you. You however have a definite need for them. Unless of course you enjoy speaking in a vacuum. Let a crowd believe it is they who are the smartest, most important people in the room and you immediately identify yourself as an inspirational speaker."
> —Steve Richards

Your Credentials

Always be willing to share your qualifications and information on your background with audience members—especially if they ask. However, a long list of your credentials is simply not required. In fact, only the following credentials will really blow an audience away:

➤ President of . . .

➤ Inventor of . . .

➤ Discoverer of . . .

➤ Author of . . .

If you're one of these, you're set. Otherwise, you should pick just two or three relevant comments about your experiences that make you a suitable presenter. The key is to make the audience trust you, not to knock them out with an amazing list of accomplishments.

If you decide to list your credentials, keep it brief and to the point. If you don't, don't worry. Your audience will respond more to the fact that you open your talk with great enthusiasm than to the fact that you mention 20 background facts about yourself. Of course, it goes without saying that you should never lie about your credentials. Once you're caught—and you will be—your audience will never believe another word you say.

One More Note: Spontaneity

Fundamental to the success of any presentation is spontaneity, and it plays an important part in your credibility equation. It also provides an opportunity to

> Join Toastmasters for the purpose of practicing and becoming more comfortable with impromptu speaking.

more fully connect with your audience. A good joke by an audience member, a piece of timely news, even a mistake you make are all spontaneous moments you can use to win the respect of your audience and strengthen your credibility with them.

There's an irony concerning spontaneity; to be spontaneous, you have to be prepared. Mark Twain once said, "It takes about six weeks to prepare a good ad lib comment." That may sound silly. But the truth is that you can plan spontaneity. Leave space for responding to the unexpected in your agenda. Never be so wed to your plan that you can't detour to go in a promising direction chosen by the audience. To respond with humor and enthusiasm shows great confidence. And to be confident is to deserve credibility!

Very Important Points To Remember

✔ Credibility flows from you to the audience. To be credible, you must inspire the audience to bestow credibility upon you.

✔ It's not enough to possess the qualities of a credible person—you must demonstrate them, both directly and indirectly, as soon as you take your place at the front of the room.

✔ You have the right to be at the front of the room. Make the audience aware that you know this, and you will gain their respect.

✔ Your credentials are important, but they will not make or break you. When discussing credentials, keep it brief. Your audience cares much more about your attitude toward them than about your resumé!

✔ Always leave room for spontaneity. It makes you look relaxed and natural in front of your audience. These characteristics build credibility.

Fill in Your Favorite Tips from the Chapter

✔ _____

_____

✔ _____

_____

This chapter reveals:

➤ The importance of setting the right tone for your presentation

➤ How tone affects the audience's perception of you

➤ How to establish a conversational tone with even the largest groups

➤ How little things affect your presentation in a big way

6

Setting the Right Tone

JEARY THEORY

The tone of your presentation affects the way your audience perceives you.

"Nothing great was ever achieved without enthusiasm."
—Ralph Waldo Emerson

The Scene . . .

You're delivering a half-day presentation to a group of 50 high-school seniors about business opportunities in your field. The presentation is being held in the high-school library, which is not an ideal place because the students may feel bored or overly comfortable due to the familiar surroundings.

As the students begin to arrive, their facial expressions suggest that they are regarding this presentation as just another class, despite the flip charts and VCR-monitor you've

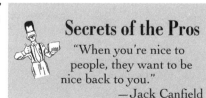

Secrets of the Pros
"When you're nice to people, they want to be nice back to you."
—Jack Canfield

113

brought in. You need to create an atmosphere that lets them know *your* presentation is something different.

The Solution ...

The solution to winning over and inspiring any audience is to set the right *tone*. The tone of your presentation—the way it feels to the audience—is the sum of everything you do. From the room you select and the clothes you wear, to the actual words you speak, you're in charge of the details. The trick is knowing how to organize them.

Secrets

1. **Tone and tonality**
   - ➤ **Presentation "tone" refers to more than your tone of voice.**
   - ➤ **The "feel" of the event creates an atmosphere.**
   - ➤ **Details are important.**

2. **Big things**
   - ➤ **Atmosphere = emotion!**
   - ➤ **Create a conversation.**
   - ➤ **Define spectrum—show "Tonometer."**
   - ➤ **Rate your own presentations!**

3. **A lot of little things are really big things**
   - ➤ **Eye contact**
   - ➤ **Word choice**
   - ➤ **Body language**
   - ➤ **Appearance**
   - ➤ **Openness**
   - ➤ **Humor**
   - ➤ **Enthusiasm**
   - ➤ **Music**
   - ➤ **Breaks**
   - ➤ **Activities**

Tone and Tonality

This word *tone* has many uses: skin tone, color tones, dial tone, tone of voice, muscle tone—virtually anything can be described in terms of its tone.

Many guides to public speaking limit themselves to discussing tone of voice when they discuss tone. What we mean, however, is the entire *impression* your audience gets from your presentation. The sum of its obvious and subtle qualities; all the big and little things taken together. Throughout the rest of this chapter, however, we use tone to refer to the way your presentation feels to audience members.

The tone of a presentation is contingent on many details that combine to give an overall impression. Was it enjoyable, inviting, user-friendly? Did participants feel welcome, interested, involved, entertained? Or were they uneasy, confused, and bored? Was the presenter conversational, accessible, confident, inspiring? Or did the presenter seem disorganized, nervous, and preachy? When we answer questions like these, we're discussing tone. The secret to using *tonality* to inspire an audience is to understand how tonality works and how to set the tone *you* want.

> ### Secrets of the Pros
> "If a presentation is long enough to use 'breaks,' get a volunteer to round up the audience."
> —Alan Jones

Always remember: *The tone of any presentation is the sum of all its details, large and small, that the audience perceives.*

Big Things

The Atmosphere of Your Presentation

Just as the atmosphere of a restaurant affects the way we perceive our dinner, so the atmosphere of a presentation affects the way we perceive the message. In both cases, consistency is the key to success.

If a restaurant has an open, fun, inviting tone, then a quiet, reserved waiter can be a letdown. If, however, you're paying big bucks for a formal meal and you get a brash, talkative waiter who likes to hang around and chat, the whole "feel" of your evening can be ruined.

In your presentations, attempt to create an atmosphere that complements your message. Decide in what atmosphere you would like to hear your own message. Consult your audience research notes (see chapter 1), and ask people familiar with your audience what atmosphere your audience is likely to enjoy. Since atmosphere is often an emotional response to surroundings, rather than a logical one, know the emotions most audiences wish to feel. As a rule, most audience members prefer the type of emotion on the left side of the following chart, including "professional audiences," which we tend to consider reserved or conservative.

Enjoyable atmosphere	Less enjoyable atmosphere
Exciting	Serious
Entertaining	Reserved
Engaging	Solitary
Relaxed	Formal
Lively	Slow
Direct	Wordy
Fun	Showy
Inviting	Closed-off
Loud	Quiet

I've listed some qualities of presenters, both good and bad. The ones on the left will almost always engage an audience and win them over.

Qualities Audiences Love	Qualities Audiences Hate
Conversational	Lecture-oriented (see below)
Open	Reserved
Accessible	Aloof
Knowledgeable	Show-off
Confident	Braggart
Entertaining	Dull
Funny	Rude or insulting
Excited to be there	Perfunctory— I've done this all before
Humility	Arrogance

Get the audience on your side by setting the right tone. Your tone can subtly say what you cannot: "I'm not perfect, so please support me." Then if something goes wrong, you'll have an audience that's willing to help you out. Coach John Wooden says, "Ask the audience for help in regard to something you appear to have forgotten." They will if you set the right tone.

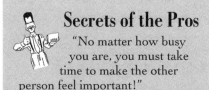

Secrets of the Pros

"No matter how busy you are, you must take time to make the other person feel important!"
—Mary Kay Ash, founder Mary Kay Cosmetics

First impressions are lasting impressions. Your audience will begin responding to you as soon as you start shaking their hands. Likewise, the surroundings you provide have an immediate impact on the atmosphere your audience perceives. Make sure the room you select sets the tone you want your audience to perceive when they arrive. The following is a checklist of details that will affect the immediate first impression your audience will have:

❑ Meeting and greeting them—are you open and inviting or aloof and removed?

❑ Type of room—a hotel conference room is different than a high school gymnasium.

❏ Lighting—full bright lights create a high-energy atmosphere.

❏ Room organization—are there boxes lying around and chairs stacked in corners, or is the room orderly and ready-to-go?

❏ Seating arrangement—does the seating encourage interaction or solitude?

For some of the larger business presentations I've helped to design, the client wished to create an atmosphere of excitement and high energy that audience members could sense immediately. The solution? High-energy music as the audience arrived and colorful, sporty banners placed throughout the room. In some cases, the presentations were delivered outdoors in large tents to increase fun and excitement. In this way, audience members could sense the carnival-like atmosphere even as they drove up. You might not have the budget for something this outrageous, but a few small things (banners and a tape deck) can have a big impact on the atmosphere of your presentation.

Create a Conversation

Always try to tailor the tone of your presentation to your specific audience. A presentation about charity fund-raising to a local high-school group will require a different tone than a marketing presentation to a group of local bank CEO's. (Though you might be surprised to find that bank CEO's are people too and like to be entertained.) The former will require a high "fun factor" (see chapter 8) and an informal atmosphere. The latter will, of course, require a more businesslike atmosphere, but not necessarily at the expense of fun. When it's all said and done, it basically comes down to a single golden rule:

> **Always attempt to create a conversational tone regardless of audience size.**

Why do people dread attending presentations almost as much as they dread giving them? Because presentations have a reputation for being boring. Presenters tend to lecture. No one wants to attend a lecture, yet most everyone enjoys a conversation. You can create a conversational tone with even the largest groups. The key is to set an inviting tone immediately—within the first three minutes.

Having a Conversation with Even the Largest Groups

Remember these tips:

➤ Try to talk *with,* not *at,* your audience.

➤ Use everyday conversational language; avoid big words.

➤ Ask questions *immediately* and listen to the answers.

➤ Get the audience involved, even if it means having them stand and shake each other's hands.

➤ Place nothing between you and your audience—avoid lecterns, podiums, and risers, when possible.

➤ Mingle with your audience; when possible, actually walk *into* the audience.

➤ Use participants' names whenever possible and encourage them to use yours.

➤ Smile—it's a natural conversation starter!

➤ Use humor.

➤ Tell stories.

Talk with, not at, your audience, and "smile a lot!" Plan to use appropriate humor. When professional facilitator David Freeborn talks with the audience about logistics, he positions it like this: "Well, folks, I've got good news and bad news. The good news is, if you are a smoker you can smoke today! The bad news is, you can't smoke in here!"

The rest of chapter 6 deals with details, big and small, that affect the tone of your presentations. But if you adopt just one piece of advice from this chapter, make it this: *create a conversation!*

Use the "Tonometer"

The tone of a presentation can be measured on a continuum between a starched and boring *lecture* and a fun and exciting *conversation*. The "Tonometer" is a gauge that helps presenters rate their presentations, while in development or even on the big day. Copy the page and keep it for yourself. You decide on which side of the tonometer your presentation will fall.

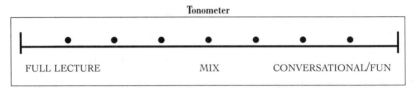

Tonometer

FULL LECTURE   MIX   CONVERSATIONAL/FUN

A Lot of Little Details Are Really Big Details

Eye Contact

Eye contact is the cement that binds a speaker and an audience. When you speak, it is your eyes that involve your listeners in your presentation, making it direct, personal, and conversational. Conversely, there is no more certain way to break the communication bond than by failing to look at your audience.

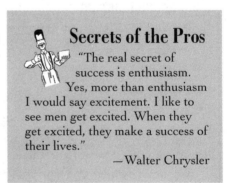

Secrets of the Pros

"The real secret of success is enthusiasm. Yes, more than enthusiasm I would say excitement. I like to see men get excited. When they get excited, they make a success of their lives."

—Walter Chrysler

No matter how large an audience may be, each listener wants to feel important, sense a personal connection with the speaker, and feel that the speaker is communicating directly with him or her. Just as a member of a small, informal group feels excluded from a conversation if the speaker doesn't meet his or her eyes, the people in your audience will feel left out if you fail to establish direct eye contact with them.

Your Words

The tone you set has a lot to do with the words you choose and the way you speak them. That's because your diction (the words you choose) and syntax (the way you put those words together) can reveal a lot about your attitude toward your audience. Remember that tone equals emotion. What your audience *feels* in your attitude toward them might as well really *be* your attitude.

The general rule on word choice is to stick close to your everyday diction. This relaxes audience members and creates that all-important conversational tone. Avoid large words—audience members may not know their meaning and they may feel you're trying to show off. Your job is not to impress the audience with your vocabulary, but rather, to communicate your message in the most entertaining, inspiring way.

Another good rule to remember is to avoid words that leave no room for dissent. These types of words beg challenges and may paint you into a corner. For example:

AVOID	USE
Always	Often, usually
Never	Seldom
Certainly	Likely
At no time	Rarely
Forever	Once in a while
Positively	Most likely

Also avoid what I call "ist" language. Language that can be taken as sexist, racist, and so on. This has less to do with political correctness than it does with the potential alienation of your audience members. Our goal is to inspire *everyone* in the room to action—100 percent buy-in. An offended or alienated audience member is *not* an inspired audience member.

121

➤ Avoid stereotypes.

➤ Don't describe people by their looks, age, race, ethnicity, or clothing.

➤ Don't say "girl" when you mean "woman."

➤ Try to use examples that equally employ both genders.

➤ Avoid tired old expressions that carry a negative connotation: "cigarette girl," "old wives' tale."

➤ Don't assume certain jobs go with a certain gender: businessman, salesman, etc.

Of course, you should never use profanity. In my opinion, avoid what you might consider even the most harmless sort of off-color language. Why? Because profanity is just that—profane. It can deeply offend audience members and there is no potential payoff that justifies the risk.

Body Language

Research has demonstrated more than half of all human communication takes place on the nonverbal level. The codes that govern nonverbal communication tend to affect us subconsciously, but are nevertheless highly efficient carriers of meaning. Each of us becomes very proficient at sending and interpreting nonverbal signals at a relatively early age. Your posture, gestures, body movements, and facial expressions are all critical nonverbal elements of your speech delivery system.

Use the following checklist:

❑ **Gestures.** Do you use your hands and your head comfortably? Are your gestures compatible with what you are saying?

❑ **Facial Expressions.** Is your face animated? Does it communicate an interest in your audience and your subject?

❑ **Posture.** Do you stand alert and erect, without being stiff? Going back on one hip, placing your hands in your pocket, pacing back and forth—all suggest that you'd rather be somewhere else.

❏ **Body Movement.** Do your movements and changes in body position serve a communicative purpose? Do they focus attention on the subject at hand?

Your Dress and Appearance

Naturally you'll want to be well-groomed for any presentation. Unless you're Albert Einstein, uncombed hair and disheveled clothing will make an audience perceive that you didn't care enough to clean up for them.

How you dress also counts. Whenever possible, dress like your audience. This will set them at ease and set an "I'm-one-of-you" tone. We live in the age of business casual—so if your audience will be in polo shirts and khaki pants, they'll feel more comfortable if you are too. If you don't know what your audience will be wearing, the general rule is to dress up a little. You can always remove a suit jacket to become less formal, but it's hard to turn jeans and a sweatshirt into business wear. The following suggestions will help:

➤ **Press your clothes.** Whenever possible, even casual clothes should be pressed. This gives an impression of crispness and neatness.

➤ **Keep your suit jacket buttoned.** Until you're ready to make a "let's roll up our sleeves and get to it" impression, button up.

➤ **Know what colors work for you.** Different colors mean different things. Loud colors can seem confident but can also seem aggressive. Darker colors can appear subdued but also dull.

Your Openness

Part of any winning tone has to do with your openness as a presenter. You can say you're open to your audience—that you're accessible, caring, and conscientious. But actions speak louder than words. Demonstrate that you are open to your audience by taking the following steps:

➤ **Ask questions regularly; then *listen* to how your audience responds.** Chapter 11 deals with question-and-answer techniques, but the following are a few pointers:

- **Listen to the entire question.**

- **Make sure you understand that the question you're hearing is the one that is being asked.**

- **Repeat the question so everyone can hear it.**

- **Don't make up an answer if you don't know the answer.**

- ***Never* put down or poke fun at an audience member's question.**

➤ **Sincerely seek audience feedback, then act on it.** If you ask your audience whether they're too cold and they say yes, you better turn the heat up.

➤ **During breaks, talk to your audience members on an individual basis.** This lets them know you're down-to-earth and accessible.

➤ **Acknowledge positive behavior and explain how it affects others.**

➤ **Ask for participants' ideas and flip chart them when possible.**

➤ **All ideas are good ideas—give compliments freely.**

➤ **Ask for comments or examples from participants.**

➤ **Talk about your own experiences.**

➤ **Don't hesitate to admit you may be wrong.**

➤ **Give complete instructions.**

Appeal to Emotion

We cannot underestimate the importance of emotion in the presentation equation. As J. P. Morgan once said, "A person usually has two reasons for doing something. One that sounds good and the real reason." That real reason is almost always based on emotion. In other words, we think with our logical faculties and act on our emotional biases.

Remember the following:

➤ **People take action based on emotion.**

➤ **Believe in what you say—say what you believe.**

➤ **Be aware of audience expression, body language, and feedback. It is a gauge of their receptivity.**

➤ **Talk with your eyes; speak from your heart.**

Humor

Humor is an international language. Everyone enjoys a laugh. But humor is more than joke telling. Funny and dynamic humor definitely generates positive energy, but

Secrets of the Pros

"If doing a long workshop, make sure you have a stool to sit on so that you maintain control even though not standing."

—Dale Ware

Jokes

A young man is sentenced to 20 years in prison and on the first day in his cell, he hears someone down the cellblock shout, "22!" Everyone within earshot, including his new cellmate, cracks up with laughter. A few minutes later, someone else shouts, "86!" Again, laughter can be heard everywhere.

"What's that all about?" the young man asks his new cellmate when the commotion has ended.

"Well, everyone's been in here so long that we've numbered our jokes," replies the old-timer. "That way instead of telling the whole thing, we can just shout the number when we want a laugh."

Being a congenial young man and eager to make friends, the young prisoner decides he'll give everyone a laugh and the next opportunity he has he shouts, "22!" Not a soul laughs. So he tries again, shouting, "86!" Dead silence. Wounded, he turns to his cellmate and asks what went wrong.

The older, wiser man pauses for a moment, then shakes his head. "Some people," he says, "just don't know how to tell a joke."

that doesn't mean you should try to be a comedian. Your goal is to present a message, and humor is another way to enhance your effectiveness.

There are two guidelines for using humor in presentations. First, share the laughter generated by the audience and second, laugh at personal mistakes. You can never go wrong by making yourself the brunt of a joke. The ability to laugh at oneself shows confidence and generosity—two

> Let's face it: HUMOR IS RISKY. The bigger the risk the bigger potential for a laugh AND the bigger potential for offending someone. Remember, they may or may not recall the joke or the laugh, but they will definitely remember if they were offended. Once you have personally offended someone, you have lost them. The trick is to maximize the laugh potential and minimize the offend potential.
>
> —Dan Finocchiaro
> Professional Trainer and
> Stand-up Comic

things that go a long way in the presentation business. The following are basic guidelines to follow when creating and using humor.

> ➤ **Use yourself as the brunt of a joke.** Avoid humor that makes you look powerful and smart. That looks like bragging and turns people off.

Secrets of the Pros

"Music is great to create an atmosphere."
—Dale Ware

> ➤ **Draw stories from real life rather than using canned jokes.**

> ➤ **If you insist on using a joke, borrow one.** Choose a joke you've seen work before groups and make sure it doesn't contain any of the potentially dangerous elements previously discussed.

> ➤ **Don't short-circuit a joke by over promising.** Never say, "I'm gonna tell you a great joke."

➤ **Don't apologize for not being a comedian.** Never preface humor with, "I'm not very funny, but here goes." It destroys the fun for everyone.

➤ **Keep it short and sweet.** Clever wording is usually short and precise. Make your humor work the same way.

➤ **Speak clearly.** A clever comment doesn't work if it has to be repeated.

Enthusiasm

Speak with enthusiasm and conviction and sincerity will follow. Studies prove that those three traits—enthusiasm, conviction, and sincerity—top the list of characteristics audiences most appreciate in a speaker. Enthusiasm is contagious, so be enthusiastic with your delivery. Psychologists tell us that people don't act, they react. Your enthusiasm will get attention and increase audience interest levels.

Aristotle, the father of rhetoric, taught that the great speaker is a good man—his convictions won't permit him to appeal to unworthy motives. So you're keeping good company when you speak with high enthusiasm. Audiences are quick to detect an unworthy attitude. They respond to the constructive and the positive. That's why speaking with wholesome conviction is admired so universally.

Enthusiasm

You can do anything if you have enthusiasm.
Enthusiasm is the yeast that makes your hopes rise to the stars.
Enthusiasm is the sparkle in your eye. It is the swing in your gait, the irresistible surge of your will and your energy to execute your ideas.
Enthusiasts are fighters.
They have fortitude.
They have staying quality.
Enthusiasm is at the bottom of all progress.
With it there is accomplishment.
Without it there are only abilities.

—Henry Ford

Setting the Right Tone

Some Smaller Details that Are Important

The following ideas can make audience members even more comfortable and set an enjoyable, conversational tone. Many of them are mentioned elsewhere in this book. But be aware that they exist and use them for your benefit!

➤ *Play some music!* Music is the universal mood setter. As a background it can underlie everything we do and say. Use music to make your presentations more exciting. High-energy, upbeat music helps set the right tone for any presentation.

➤ *Take frequent breaks!* Sitting still is hard work for adults. It's best to provide frequent breaks—at least one every sixty to ninety minutes. Also, an audience member who desperately needs to use the restroom or stretch his or her legs is definitely not paying 100 percent attention to what you have to say. Always set a specific time to return and start back up. (See chapter 10 for more on breaks.)

➤ *Don't hesitate to use activities!* Activities get the audience up and moving. Even the most somber group of business people respond to fun and appropriate activities that make a point. People remember 10 percent of what they read, 20 percent of what they hear, 30 percent of what they hear and see—and up to 80 percent of what they hear, see, and do. Get them involved by using Business Entertainment™. (See chapter 8 for more details.)

Very Important Points to Remember

✔ The tone you establish determines how the audience perceives you; if they approve, you will get 100 percent *buy-in*.

✔ Everything counts when you're establishing *tone*. Know how to create the right atmosphere.

✔ Create a conversational tone—no matter what the occasion!

✔ People respond to emotion. Make sure everything you say and do works both intellectually and emotionally.

Fill in Your Favorite Tips from the Chapter

✔ _____
_____

✔ _____
_____

✔ _____
_____

✔ _____
_____

✔ _____
_____

✔ _____
_____

✔ _____
_____

✔ _____
_____

✔ _____
_____

✔ _____
_____

✔ _____
_____

✔ _____
_____

✔ _____
_____

Setting the Right Tone

This chapter reveals:

➤ The importance of doing more than is expected in your presentations

➤ How to set and exceed expectations

➤ How to use your audience members' names

➤ How to make audience members the stars of your presentation

7

Exceeding Expectations

JEARY THEORY

In order to exceed expectations, you must understand your audience—know what they want. Then deliver more!

"When we do more than we are paid to do, eventually we will be paid more for what we do."

—Zig Ziglar, speaker and author

The Scene...

You're not exactly a beginner at making presentations—you know how to get an audience excited and how to deliver what they expect.

But now you want to do something extra that just blows the audience away.

But there's so much to remember just getting your presentation up and running. How are you ever going to remember those little extras that please audiences so much?

Secrets of the Pros

"An audience expects you to do a good job— that's customer satisfaction. It's those 'little extras' you do that can make your presentation memorable and create 'customer delight.'"

—David Freeborn

131

The Solution . . .

Up to this point, we've discussed what your presentation must have to make it successful. If you simply follow the steps and bulleted points outlined in the previous chapters, you'll be well on your way to having successful presentations. But you can virtually ensure 100 percent audience buy-in that leads to true inspiration by going a few steps further.

Often audiences respond as well when they receive small things they didn't expect as they do when they receive the big things they did expect. Become known as a presenter who delivers that little *something extra*.

Secrets

1. Give value—do more than is expected.

2. Know your audience's wants, needs, and desires.

3. Establish expectations early in the presentation.

   ➤ Define what the presentation is and isn't.

   ➤ Define what it can and can't do.

   ➤ Define your role (facilitator, expert, entertainer, trainer, etc.).

4. Under promise, over deliver.

5. Learn and use names.

   ➤ Using name badges properly makes a big difference.

   ➤ Know what to do with nicknames.

   ➤ Memorize a few names to get started.

6. Create winning opportunities for your audience.

7. Always hold a little back in reserve.

   ➤ Keep deliverables in reserve—have several aces in the hole to surprise the audience.

8. Prepare those little extras—examples of what you have to offer.

Give Value — Do More Than Is Expected

The one thing we all have in common is that we love to get a little bit more than we paid for. It can be almost anything—an extra few hours of commitment, a card that sums up the points of a presentation, even pictures of an event or presentation.

I would say that 90 percent of all the effort I put into a job is making sure I deliver what the client wants. I can almost always make my client happy by delivering what was paid for. But by adding an extra 10 percent, I can have a completely thrilled client. Guess what the client will remember most: the 90 percent that went into making sure they remember what they asked for or the 10 percent that went into the little extras?

The same is true for your presentations. When someone hires you (or invites you or accepts your offer to volunteer) as a presenter, they expect you to communicate a message to an audience. Once they arrive, your audience expects this as well. The bad news is this: Everyone pretty much takes for granted all the effort you put into making a presentation. Audiences expect the room to be in order, the tone to be inviting, and the speaker to be prepared and entertaining.

Here's the great news: Once you've covered those basics, you can blow your audience away by adding a few little extras that will make them remember your presentation for years to come. The way to do this is to make sure you really know what they want, then figure out a way to give a little more while they aren't looking.

Know Your Audience's Deepest Needs and Desires

If you have analyzed your audience, you'll have a clear idea of what they want. From the beginning, your presentation should be geared to the particular audience to which you are speaking. It doesn't matter if they are car salespeople, ministers, or lawyers—audiences are people too. This means they have a whole host of needs, desires, and wants that go far beyond the topic you're there to talk about. In addition to their obvious conscious desire to be entertained and

133

informed in an open, inviting, and comfortable atmosphere (see chapters 2 through 6), audiences also have at least *seven* subtle and unconscious desires. Everyone wishes:

1. **To belong**

2. **To be respected**

3. **To be appreciated and liked**

4. **To be safe**

5. **To be successful**

6. **To find romance**

7. **To be enthused**

This is not to say that you can (or should even try to) meet and exceed all seven of these subconscious desires. You should be well aware of them however. When you deliver the extras that please audiences, you'll be aiming at those subconscious and emotional desires much more than at the conscious and rational ones I mentioned earlier.

Little Things Sell Big Things

If you want someone to buy something big, toss in a small extra free. A friend of mine, John Bacon, calls it the "Cracker Jack"™ syndrome. Not everybody buys a box of Cracker Jack™ for the caramel corn and peanuts, however delicious you might think they are. Some buy it for that little 2 cent prize at the bottom.

Another friend remembers buying his first new car, which represented a huge investment for him. While showing it off to his next-door neighbor, he opened the glove box and found a pair of brown cotton gloves with an attached note scrawled on the back of the salesman's business card. "These are in case you ever have to change a tire," he had written. My friend remembers the $1.50 pair of gloves, though he now has a hard time remembering the price of that car.

As I pointed out in chapter 6, human beings think with their rational minds, but act on (and remember) emotions. If you deliver little extras, your audience will be more likely to buy-in to the big things you came to deliver.

Establish Expectations Early in the Presentation

One mistake you can make is failing to agree on a reasonable level of expectation early in the presentation. Although it doesn't have to be within the first three minutes (see chapter 4), you shouldn't wait long to ask your audience to describe their expectations. The following *three-step* process almost always works for me:

1. **Outline *your* expectations for the day.** I do this by revealing my objectives, the topic and main ideas I will cover, as well as the agenda.

2. **Make three commitments up front.** I commit to delivering 1) valuable, usable information; 2) as excellent a presentation as I can; and 3) fun. For these three commitments, I ask the audience to make one commitment: to get involved.

3. **Ask the audience for *their* expectations.** I write these in one- or two-word bullet points on a flip chart, then review them, pointing out which expectations are realistic and which are not.

Not only does this system put the audience in the driver's seat, it also results in a page that "puts everything on the table" and allows us to fine-tune and come to agreement on what the presentation can and cannot do. If you use this approach, it will serve as a sort of contract between you and the audience and guarantees that you will come a long way toward meeting their expectations — because they're clearly defined for everyone to see.

Early in any presentation, most presenters feel a strong urge to make big promises that will excite their audiences. Not a bad idea — as long as they can deliver the goods. The problem is, the tendency to exaggerate a little. In so doing, we set ourselves up for failure the way a high jumper does when he sets the bar too high. Nowhere is this urge to promise big as strong as when you discuss objectives and expectations with the audience.

Remember this rule: *under promise and over deliver.*

Under Promise, Over Deliver

Making promises we can't keep is a bad habit. Often in our everyday lives, we're tempted to promise things we know will be difficult—whether it's to spend more time with our families, deliver something at work, or meet a friend. Sometimes the reason we do this is because promising is easier than facing the truth—that we might not have time to get the job done or don't want to meet the friend. Try to remember the times you've been in a jam for promising more than you could deliver!

The temptation to promise more than you can deliver in a presentation is at least as strong as in everyday life. After all, you can really dazzle your audience with an opener that promises to answer all their questions, keep them entertained, and make them rich. However, audiences are shrewd. They'll start to catch on quickly that you're not backing up your promises—that you're failing to deliver value. Once that happens, you'll have a hard time keeping your credibility level high. Solve this problem by not promising too much. If you keep the level of expectation within reason—by not over promising—your audience will be thrilled when they get *more* than they expected!

Avoid Promising Too Much

Over promising is like charging up a credit card. It feels good for a moment but later you have to pay up—sometimes more than you can afford. Don't fall into the trap! The following are a few common situations where the temptation to over promise is strong:

➤ **Promising more value than you can deliver.** Don't say, "By the time you're done with this presentation, you'll know more about this topic than your bosses do." Try this, "I promise to use all the skill I have to make this information easy to understand and this presentation fun!"

➤ **Promising things you can't control.** Don't promise a great lunch or an early ending time or great future success.

➤ **Promising things will occur at specific times.** Don't promise lunch will be at noon. If it's ten minutes late, you have failed.

Under promise by saying we'll get to lunch as early as possible, depending on how much material we cover. No one will know lunch was ten minutes late.

➤ **When asked when the presentation is scheduled to end, be conservative in your estimate.** Even people who want to listen to you like to know when the talk will end. Create your presentations so that you have plenty of extra time. If you know your talk will last until 2:00 p.m., announce that you plan to close at 3:00 p.m. If you finish ten minutes *late*, your audience will feel they are getting out fifty minutes *early*.

➤ **Building up jokes or segments of your talk beyond what you can realistically deliver.** Many a good joke has been killed by the buildup. When you say, "Let me tell you the funniest joke I ever heard in my life," you set the bar very high indeed. Just tell the joke. An unexpected bit of humor is always better than an expected one. Likewise, use short transitions between sections of your talk. Avoid the temptation to "build up" the next topic you're going to talk about.

Learn and Use Names

Names are powerful tools and far too few presenters take advantage of them. When you use someone's name, you have acknowledged that person's specialness. Since most people have trouble remembering and using names, they don't expect others — even speakers and presenters — to have that ability. For that very reason, names provide a great opportunity to impress your audience and deliver that extra touch that inspires them.

Some speakers have the power to remember the names of everyone in a room without the use of name badges or other props. If you're one of those people — congratulations! Your job has just become a whole lot easier. If you're like the rest of us — take heart. Most audience members will have a difficult time remembering your name and won't expect you to remember or use theirs.

Exceeding Expectations

Memorizing Names

Learning the names of 50 or even 100 people in a few minutes might seem like magic, but it isn't. The key is to meet each audience member *individually*, before the presentation. Get their names, one by one, and commit them to memory. If this sounds ridiculous, consider how many people you know — by name and face. It's likely to be in the thousands (even higher, if you include famous names and faces of people you've never met). Adding a few more isn't that difficult, but it does takes concentration.

My friend John Bacon has the uncanny knack of remembering the names of every person in a room. I asked him how he does it, and he passed along these tips.

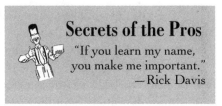

Secrets of the Pros

"If you learn my name, you make me important."
—Rick Davis

➤ **Meet each audience member as soon as possible.** Make eye contact with that person and shake hands. When you ask for his or her name — *listen*! I mean *really* listen.

➤ **Repeat the name at least twice.** "Good morning, Joe. Nice to meet you. Come on in and have a seat, Joe."

➤ **As you survey the room before your talk begins, silently remind yourself of each person's name.** "That's Joe, that's Mary." Don't be afraid to ask for the name once or twice more. And don't be afraid to ask a few questions of audience members, using their names liberally while you're doing so.

You'll be shocked how easily you can master names and faces even in a large group. Use names whenever possible, but remember to do so appropriately.

Use first names when:

➤ Calling on someone with a question.

➤ Repeating that person's question for the rest of the group to hear.

➤ Answering a question someone has asked.

➤ Praising someone or offering a compliment.

➤ Asking someone to join you at the front of the room.

Secrets of the Pros

"Make sure any group you are working with has name tags—this allows you to call them by name."

—Dale Ware

Whenever possible, try to get a list of names in advance so you can practice pronouncing them. Nothing sends a signal that you don't care faster than mispronouncing a name. If in doubt, ask for the correct pronunciation—then use it!

Know How To Use Name Badges

The next-best thing to memorizing every name in the room is to use name badges (depending on the size of your audience). They are a powerful tool, but too often they are used incorrectly. For example, audience members are usually handed a blank sticker upon which to scrawl their own names. Remember, when you really *need* the name is when you're at the front of the room presenting. If name badges are written in different handwriting and with different pens, you'll never be able to read them. A little pre-planning provides easy solutions to the problem. Consider these tips:

➤ **Whenever possible, use prepared name badges.** These can be written out by hand ahead of time, using a list of audience members. Or you can type the names on a sheet of paper and slide them into clip-on name badge sleeves available at most office-supply stores.

➤ **The first name is the one you'll need when you're at the front of the room.** When you prepare name tags, place the first name above (rather than before) the last name, center the first name and put it in larger print than the last name.

| **Right way** | **Wrong way** |

➤ **Keep blank name tags on hand.** If you spell someone's name incorrectly, they will probably say it's OK. IT IS NOT OK! Get rid of the misspelled name badge immediately and prepare a new one. Names are powerful. Never misspell them!

➤ **If you are using hand-printed name tags, print them yourself or have an assistant print them as audience members arrive.** This provides a standard printing style and a more legible name tag.

➤ **Ask audience members to keep their name tags in plain view.**

➤ **Wear a badge with your name on it.** Be one of them!

A Thought on Nicknames

There are two schools of thought on nicknames. Many presenters use them liberally and, I think, presumptuously. Other presenters use them only after they've been invited to use them. You can probably guess which group I'm in.

In general, an audience member will let you know if she prefers a nickname to her given name. If so, use it. And if you're using a preprinted name badge with the audience member's formal name, write a new one.

If the name badge says "William," then he is not "Will," "Bill," "Billy," or any other variation unless that's what he asks you to call him. If William Shakespeare walked into your presentation, you wouldn't want to be remembered as the person who called him Bill all day long.

How To Have a One-On-One Conversation with 500 People at the Same Time

I was presenting to a large convention in New Orleans. There were about 500 people in the room and I was doing a 90-minute presentation on communications skills. It was early in my career as a speaker and I was dutifully looking over the entire room, making eye contact here and there and making sure no one felt left out.

After the presentation was over, several people thanked me for the attention I had given them during the talk. They all said, "I felt like you were talking to me personally." That's why the talk was so good. It impressed me, because even though I was making eye contact I was not speaking to anyone in particular. I learned from that one event the single most important lesson I ever learned about audiences. Make your talk a one-on-one conversation—just do it with several hundred people at the same time.

—Bob Gerold

Create Winning Opportunities for Your Audience

A good friend of mine has a phrase he repeats before each presentation, "Let your audience be the hero." Audience members are like everyone else on the planet, they wish to be respected, seen as intelligent, and praised in front of their peers. Use this information to make sure your audience members feel as if they are "winning" when they listen to your presentations.

Level One Opportunities

Level One winning opportunities are those moments that simply occur—an audience member tells a funny joke, asks a good question, or answers a question as well as or better than you could. In these instances, repeat the comment, wisecrack, question, or answer so the entire group can hear it and then *praise the audience member.* Never underestimate the power of praise and encouragement. An impromptu winning opportunity such as this will accomplish the following:

➤ **Make the individual you point out feel great.**

➤ Reduce the anxiety audience members feel about joining in when they see that you will recognize their efforts.

➤ **Create greater audience buy-in.** Audiences are willing to meet you halfway if you pay attention to them.

➤ **Create a feeling of pride and ownership among audience members** when they see that you endorse what they say.

Level Two Opportunities

Level Two winning opportunities are those that you create. This includes asking questions that audience members can answer — then letting them answer the questions fully. When an audience member answers one of your questions correctly, all sorts of great things happen. For one thing, the audience member feels good about himself and will want to answer more of your questions. Other audience members will then want to jump on the bandwagon, creating a good dynamic between you and the audience.

The following are a few ways you might create winning opportunities for your audience:

➤ **Get audience members involved.** Assign them bits of information, then let *them* deliver the information during your presentation.

➤ **Ask for volunteers from the group to help you make a point.** Magicians use audience members as helpers to create credibility and audience buy-in — so should you!

➤ **Call for applause when an audience member comes to the front of the room.** Don't embarrass them with applause when they merely answer a question correctly. But when they assist you in some way (writing on flip charts, delivering a set of bullet points), remember to say something like, "How about a nice hand for James."

➤ **Always give credit to the audience.** Don't make the mistake of telling an audience member's joke as if you made it up. Be sure to repeat comments so others can hear them — then give those people credit so the group can see that you are fair and will reward any risks they take.

The object is to make your audience members feel like "heroes" by drawing attention to them rather than to yourself. They'll remember your presentation because they (not you) were the center of attention.

Always Hold a Little Back in Reserve

It's a good idea to always hold back a small surprise for your audience while you're giving a presentation. This can be just about anything—a joke, some giveaways, a piece of information they didn't think they would get, an early departure time, a laminated card with the five top points of your presentation on it. The key is surprise. A magician's tricks work because he doesn't let the audience know exactly what's going to happen until it happens.

If you plan to hold something back in order to surprise your audience, you may be tempted to let the cat out of the bag. Don't! Hold your trump card back so that you can wow your audience when they least expect it. Just as timing is all-important to a magician or comedian, knowing what to hold back is equally important. Remember, most of the fun in a surprise isn't what you get so much as the delight that someone went to the trouble of surprising you!

Some of the Extras You Might Prepare:

❑ Scented markers

❑ Specially prepared handouts

❑ Comical overheads

❑ Laminated cards with your (or better, the audience's) words written out

❑ Funny handouts, pictures, and recordings

❑ Pens, pins

❑ Simple handouts summing up what you've covered

The idea is to deliver these extras with a little pizzazz. Don't ruin the surprise by telling the audience what you have in mind. Allow your audience the pleasure of a surprise and the opportunity to see

143

you as someone who goes beyond mere expectations. Remember, a little goes a long way, so don't make things too hard for yourself by promising too much!

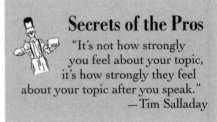

Secrets of the Pros

"It's not how strongly you feel about your topic, it's how strongly they feel about your topic after you speak."
—Tim Salladay

One Last Word: Remain Flexible

Most audiences don't expect much flexibility from presenters. Surprise them by being the kind of person who can meet them halfway. Changing the order of your presentation, adding or removing something, or taking an unscheduled break all signal flexibility.

Even moving your presentation to another room or outdoors can be the little something extra that makes an audience remember your presentation. Don't be afraid to experiment.

Very Important Points To Remember

✔ Everyone loves something extra. Know your audience and their expectations, then exceed those expectations.

✔ Hold a little back so that you can provide "little extras" that wow your audience.

✔ Create winning opportunities for your audience—make your audience the hero!

✔ Most audiences expect dry, dull presentations. Exceed expectations by learning your audience's names, speaking in plain English, and using humor.

Fill in Your Favorite Tips from the Chapter

✔ _____
_____

✔ _____
_____

PART 3
The Body of Your Presentation

This chapter reveals:

➤ The difference between how presenters speak and audiences think, and what that means to you

➤ How to create "peaks of interest" throughout your presentation

➤ How to heat up your presentation by gaining and maintaining audience involvement

➤ How to use "Business Entertainment™" to keep your audience on the edge of their seats

8

Keeping Their Attention

JEARY THEORY

Because the average adult has an attention span of five to seven minutes, you should manage your presentations in a way that gets your point across and keeps your audience at the highest possible level of interest.

"People will pay more to be entertained than educated."
—Johnny Carson

The Scene...

Your presentation started out with energy and excitement. But now that you've gotten into the nitty-gritty, you can sense that your audience's energy level is ebbing. The facts and figures you're presenting are pertinent and your audience should be interested, but they just aren't motivated anymore. How do you get your audience back to the level of excitement they were at during the first three minutes of your presentation?

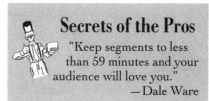

Secrets of the Pros

"Keep segments to less than 59 minutes and your audience will love you."
—Dale Ware

The Solution . . .

You must understand how your audience's attention span works.

The average adult has an attention span of five to seven minutes. That's the reason commercial breaks in prime-time TV programming last about three to four minutes and most pop songs rarely go longer than five or six minutes. Even with multisensory stimulation (that is, getting information not only by hearing words, but also by seeing, feeling, smelling, or tasting), the presenter can still only count on the average person's attention for five to seven minutes.

If the brevity of the adult attention span is problematic for television producers and songwriters, it's a veritable nightmare for the presenter. Five to seven minutes is barely enough time to walk to the front of the room and inform your audience about the day's subject matter.

Considering the fact that even a short presentation lasts about an hour, overcoming the challenge of your audience's attention span is a real problem. But it gets worse . . . .

The average presenter speaks at about 120 to 200 words per minute. The average listener, however, can comprehend between 600 and 800 words per minute. This means your audience is thinking about *four times faster than* you can give them information to think about. That gives your audience's collective mind plenty of time to race ahead of you. Couple this with your audience's five- to seven-minute attention span and what you've got—if you're not careful—is a room full of people miles away from you and your presentation.

The good news is that your audience will have a high level of interest in the first few minutes of your presentation. They will be "feeling" you out and trying to decide whether your presentation is worth listening to. The other natural "attention spike" occurs as soon as you utter the words, "in closing." As soon as the audience realizes the presentation is nearly over, they're awake again. The problem is keeping their interest in that vast attention-span desert between the beginning and end.

The following are some secrets to ensure that your audience will be as fresh and interested at the conclusion as they were the moment your presentation began.

Secrets

1. **Use Business Entertainment™ to keep your audience interested**. All audiences have natural highs and lows, so keep your audience excited by including a jolt of Business Entertainment™ every five to seven minutes.

2. **Know when and how to use the following Business Entertainment™ crowd pleasers:**

   ➤ **Music**

   ➤ **Games**

   ➤ **Stories**

   ➤ **Activities**

   ➤ **Skits**

   ➤ **Give away freebies**

Business Entertainment™

Business Entertainment™ is a concept I've been using for some time. If you want to grab

Secrets of the Pros

"Do use props, demonstrations, activities to let audience 'experience' key points. Don't just use lecture . . . boring, puts people to sleep."

your audience's attention and keep it, you need to use hooks and different types of attention grabbers *throughout your presentation*. Remember, they are thinking way ahead of what you're saying.

Research supports the common sense behind Business Entertainment™. For years psychologists have maintained that the adult attention span is *increased* and learning *enhanced* by:

➤ **An uninhibited environment**

➤ **Creative approaches to solving problems**

➤ **Allowing mistakes to be made**

➤ Constructive and timely feedback

➤ Experiential learning (that is, doing instead of hearing)

And here's another interesting set of statistics. The average adult *retains:*

➤ 10% of what he or she reads

➤ 20% of what he or she hears

➤ 30% of what he or she sees

➤ 50% of what he or she hears and sees

➤ 70% of what he or she says . . . and

➤ 90% of what he or she says and does

That means if you want your audience to become inspired by, and act on one out of ten words you say, give them a lecture and make them listen. If, on the other hand, you want to inspire your audience with nine out of ten words you say, get them saying and doing it *themselves*. That's Business Entertainment™!

Another approach to the same problem is practiced by presentation guru David Peoples. He calls his solution "Hot Spice," and his book, *Presentations Plus*, is worth reading. Peoples says that by adding a dash of "hot spice" to your talk every six to eight minutes, you achieve a "funnel" of attention and interest that allows you to get the information into the minds of your audience. It's a little different approach, but if it works, try it!

Using Business Entertainment™

Now that you know the *why* behind Business Entertainment™, let's take a minute to cover the *how*. Remember, we're trying to solve two problems at once. First, the human mind has a tendency to wander during a lecture, retaining very little of what is heard. Second, even an engaging activity will lose its appeal for the average person after a period of time.

That means Business Entertainment™ has *three* goals:

1. **To break up the monotony of your speaking voice by employing some activity, event, point, change, or other eye-opener.**

2. **To jolt the audience and make your point by selecting an eye-opener that uses something other than words.** Ideally it should involve the audience saying and doing.

3. **To add a "fun factor."**

This will revitalize your audience during the natural lows in their attention span and increase their retention. The following are some of the activities and eye-openers you might consider using.

Games, Skits, Activities, and Other Audience-Involvers

Games, skits, and activities are simply the best types of Business Entertainment™. Why? Because they get the audience up and moving, saying and doing. And a little friendly competition *really* wakes up the room.

When using a game or activity, make sure you set the game up properly. Clearly explain the rules of the game and write them on a flip chart or a handout. Then *get involved yourself.* This will signal to the audience that they can let go and enjoy the activity.

The following are several simple rules to keep in mind when designing games and activities:

1. **Always choose an energizing activity.**

2. **Make sure the game relates to the point you're trying to illustrate.**

3. **Pacing is the name of the activity game.** It's better to run a short, quick-moving game and have the audience return to their seats laughing, energized, and wanting more than to draw out an activity and risk a loss of impact.

Secrets of the Pros

"Have fun while you are onstage. If you have fun, it is guaranteed they will have fun."

—Tony Walker

Music

Nonverbal information is powerful to the eye—and to the ear. We spend a lot of time making sure we signal our interest to audience members through careful body language, well-developed visuals, and so on. But we tend to neglect the other powerful sense at work during a presentation: hearing. The audience needs a break from your voice. And a good way to provide this is with music.

Music sets a mood and creates an atmosphere. Use different types of music for different effects. It's wise to take several types of CD's with you, and don't hesitate to ask the audience which types they enjoy. The beginning and end of your presentation, as well as during breaks, are especially good times to use music.

Verbal Surveying

Keep your audience interested by keeping them involved! Don't *tell them* every key point, ask them to *tell you* after each exercise. This

Hatfields and McCoys

An example of the sort of activity you might use to energize a medium-sized group—and review material, as well—is an activity that David Freeborn calls the "Hatfields and McCoys." It's a question-and-answer game that works effectively to energize the audience and increase their retention. Divide the room into two equal groups. One group will be the Hatfields, the other the McCoys—and the presenter will be Da Judge. Da Judge will ask questions and each team will compete to answer.

There are only a couple of rules to the game. First, your audience members must jump to their feet and raise a hand to be recognized before giving an answer. Second, Da Judge is never wrong. A little friendly competition gets the room really going. You can keep score, play for prizes, or play just for the fun of it. Use your imagination! The key to the Hatfields and McCoys, as with all games and activities, is to keep it brief enough to make your audience want to come back for more.

results in more participation, heightened credibility, and confirmation that they have indeed received the message.

You want your audience members to leave the session impressed with how much *they* know, rather than how much *you* know. In fact, several times during your presentation, you should simply survey the audience out loud. Ask audience members about the pace of your presentation, how useful the content is, even the room temperature. The response will allow you to adjust as you make your audience comfortable and, of course, better able to really buy-in to your message.

Stories and Anecdotes

Stories and anecdotes create interest and add spice to your presentation. Be careful though, audiences won't appreciate stories that are not related to the topic. In general, your stories should do one of *three* things: illustrate a point, create humor, or relate your experience to your audience's experiences. Also, allowing audience members to tell their own stories is a good way to create rapport and audience involvement.

Some Rules for Using Stories as Business Entertainment™

➤ **Keep them short.** As I once heard a speaker say, "Don't tell me where you bought the matches, just tell me how big the fire was."

➤ **Make them illustrate a point.** Audiences don't want to hear about your generic experiences or observations. Relate the story to the point you are making.

➤ **Use your own experience.** Whenever possible, your stories should relate your own experiences rather than secondhand experience. This makes the story immediate and credible.

> **Secrets of the Pros**
>
> "When the number of awards is high, it makes the perceived possibility of winning something high as well. And then the average man will stretch to achieve."
>
> —Tom Peters

153

Videos

Audiences retain up to 50 percent of what they see *and* hear, so videos and other audiovisual equipment add emphasis to your message. When using videos, enhance your audience's attention by taking a few minutes to set up what they're going to see. Give them a couple of hints about points to look for or ask them to jot down two or three things they have learned. This will focus their attention and keep them actively involved as opposed to just passively watching.

For an in-depth outline of how to use video equipment and other tools of the presentation trade, see chapter 9.

Taking Breaks

Breaks are also natural energizers. You can't take them every five to seven minutes (no matter how much audience members may wish you could), but you can take them frequently. To focus audience attention, keep the breaks short or provide them with break activities—something to think or talk about for discussion when they return. You can also use breaks as opportunities to survey the audience and see what's working and what isn't. Remember the following tips:

➤ **Schedule breaks every 60 to 90 minutes.**

➤ **Be flexible.** You may need breaks to be *more* or *less* frequent.

➤ **Know break logistics.** The location of restrooms, smoking areas, phones, and refreshments is vitally important.

➤ **Create a break policy.** Be sure to inform the audience at the beginning of your presentation.

➤ **Manage breaks.** Settle on a return time (e.g., "Let's return at 10:10 a.m.") rather than a length of time (such as, "Let's take ten minutes").

➤ **Use gimmicks and prompts.** These are a great way to alert audience members that breaks are ending (train whistle, music prompts, etc.).

Freebies

If it works at the beginning (see chapter 4), it will work in the middle. Give something away!

I realized this when I was giving a presentation in Denver with a partner. It was in the middle of a day-long presentation, and we had covered all our morning material. Searching for something to divert our audience, my partner turned to a box of pens—something we were saving for later in our program. He started reviewing the morning's material by asking the audience random questions and tossing Bic™ pens around the room. The audience roared back to life! For the rest of the week, we made sure we had pens for each new audience.

The items you give away don't have to be expensive, just unexpected and free. The following are a few good ideas for freebies you can carry with you.

➤ **Pens, pins, ball caps, or other trinkets that carry your organization's name on it.**

➤ **Cassette tapes, videotapes, booklets of your own material, or that of others who might otherwise interest your audience.** Always include your business card.

➤ **Candy is always well received.** Be careful to include a variety of chocolate and non-chocolate candies, as well as sugared and sugar-free, so everyone can participate.

➤ **Use a camera to take pictures of audience members engaged in activities, then give them copies of the photographs.** They make nice gifts, and they will always have it to remind them of your presentation.

➤ **Provide a simple handout summing up your major points.**

➤ **Money.** Ok, call me simple. But I like to give away money, a dollar at a time. I have fifty fresh dollar bills gum-bound to a cardboard backing. I call them "Texas Scratch Pads," and every

time an audience member does something out of the ordinary—
makes a humorous remark, adds value to the day, volunteers for
an activity—he or she gets a buck. Audience members love this,
and it's always worth the extra few dollars I spend.

Note Taking

Although we sometimes forget what we hear, retention soars
when we reinforce it by writing it down. Take, for example, a
shopping list. Even when we forget to take it with us, we often
"see" what we wrote on the list. The act of writing "imprinted"
the list in our memory.

In many of my train-the-trainer seminars, I use the "Very
Important Point" concept. Virtually all presentations contain too
much information for the audience to readily absorb. So I ask my
audiences to take notes—but notes with a twist. Rather than telling
them what to write, I allow them to choose the material that seems
important to them. Occasionally I review, just to prove to them
how much they are picking up. When asking your audience to take
notes, remember these rules:

➤ *Suggest*, **don't order, note taking.** Try saying, "Here's an idea
you might jot down."

➤ **Help attendees by sifting through the information.** Ask that
they jot down only the top *three* points that seem useful to them.

➤ **Pause to give your audience time to take notes.**

One Last Note

The idea behind Business Entertainment™ is to keep even the
most reserved groups energized and interested. You should strive
to keep a fun, inviting, and risk-free environment during any
activity and throughout the presentation. Make sure everyone gets
and feels involved. Remember, a little healthy competition and
creativity go a long way. Keep your audiences interested by keeping
them entertained!

Very Important Points To Remember

✔ Audience members have an attention span of five to seven minutes. Keep them hooked by giving them a jolt of Business Entertainment™ at their natural attention lows.

✔ Audiences think faster than you can speak. Keep them occupied by providing sources of input other than spoken words.

✔ Games and other energizers work best when they are well-explained, quickly paced, and short.

✔ Everyone enjoys Business Entertainment™, but be sure to tailor your activities and diversions to the specific audience.

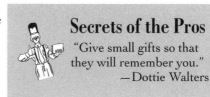

Secrets of the Pros

"Give small gifts so that they will remember you."
—Dottie Walters

Fill in Your Favorite Tips from the Chapter

✔ _____
_____

✔ _____
_____

✔ _____
_____

I often develop courses in which time is allowed for participants to break out into groups of two to seven people. I ask each group to note on a flip chart what they believe are the best points of the presentation. Then I have each group share its best points with the other groups.

This chapter reveals:

➤ How to view the room as a tool

➤ What types of visual aids are available and
   the advantages and disadvantages of each

➤ How to select visual aids for your presentation

➤ How to use tools like a pro

9

Using the Tools of the Trade

JEARY THEORY

To fully engage an audience and increase information retention, use as much variety as time and budget allow.

"Things seen are mightier than things heard."
—Alfred Lord Tennyson

The Scene...

You now know that the greatest impact is made when people not only hear your words, but see them as well, and do it all in a comfortable atmosphere. But there's a whole world of media out there—everything from flip charts and markers to overhead projectors, TVs and VCRs, and interactive computer equipment. What you need is a guide to sort through everything that's available and show you what to use—and how and when to use it.

The Solution...

Turn to the handy toolbox on page 175. Presenters use dozens of tools in many different ways to enhance their messages, ensure audience buy-in, and increase audience retention. Your only limitations are your own knowledge of the tools available and how to use them. After that, your imagination's the limit.

Secrets

1. **Tools are everywhere; know when and how to use them.**

2. **The room is the most overlooked tool a presenter has.**

3. **Visual aids are the secret to success**
   - ➤ **Why we use them**
   - ➤ **When we use them**
   - ➤ **How we use them**

4. **Types of tools:**
   - ➤ **Flip charts**
   - ➤ **Overhead and slide projectors**
   - ➤ **Handouts**
   - ➤ **TV/VCR (videos)**
   - ➤ **Props**
   - ➤ **Twenty-first-century tools: CDI and computers**
   - ➤ **Presenter's toolbox**

Tools

The New World Dictionary defines a tool as "any instrument or device necessary to one's profession or occupation." I would expand that to "any tool or device that makes one's occupation (or life, for that matter) a little easier and more effective."

Like most trades, the presentation business has a lot of tools to master and there are rules and guidelines for using them effectively. I'd like to spend some time discussing one of the most critical—and often overlooked—tools of the presentation trade.

The Room: The Most Overlooked of All Your Tools

Until now you might have taken the room for granted. After all, it's pretty much just a room, right? Wrong! The room is perhaps the single most important tool you have as a presenter. The sooner you learn to use it to your advantage, the better.

Room Size

When it comes to rooms, the right size counts. A room that is too large makes the audience feel uneasy and lonely. It also places a lot of weight on your shoulders. You have to fill that void with lights, sound, and action. Likewise, a room that's too small makes your presentation feel cramped.

The right size is one where everyone can relax in their seats and get up and move around without bumping elbows. If you must choose one over the other, however, go with a slightly smaller room. This ensures that your presentation will seem well-attended and everyone gets to know everyone else. Remember the following:

➤ **Your room should be the correct size for your audience.**

➤ **Your room should be comfortable.**

➤ **Large rooms and those with high ceilings are often cold and have a tendency to produce distracting echoes.**

Room Shape

The shape of the room is equally important. The audience must be able to see you, your visual aids, and, ideally, each other. Try to avoid the following:

➤ **Rooms with structural supports that block the view.**

➤ **Rooms with deep recesses—unless people can sit there, it's a waste of space.**

The Rules of the Room

The following are tips that will help you create and maintain an inspiring environment for your presentation:

➤ **Arrange your seating according to what you want to accomplish.**

➤ Ensure that every audience member will be able to see and hear without straining.

➤ Know where to find the lighting controls, and how to use them.

➤ Know where to find the heating and cooling controls, and who to call if you can't adjust them yourself.

➤ Familiarize yourself with your room's furnishings and how they work: window shades, microphones, etc.

➤ Use comfortable chairs whenever possible.

➤ Consider the number, location, and size of screens, monitors, and flip charts.

➤ Use a microphone for audiences of more than 50 whenever possible.

➤ Decide whether you need a stage (or riser) in a hotel.

➤ Have the seating arrangement wide and flat rather than narrow and deep, whenever possible.

Once your room is set up, you'll be ready to fill it with the excitement and enthusiasm of your presentation.

Windows

Natural lighting is terrific but as a rule, avoid windows. You have enough distractions to contend with. Why invite audience members to stare at the world as it passes by. Another problem is the sun. Nothing is more distracting and uncomfortable than having bright, hot sunshine in your face while you're trying to listen—much less trying to speak. Also, the sun plays havoc with visual equipment, especially VCR's and television monitors, which can fade out if bright light falls on them.

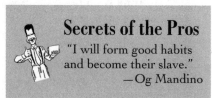

Secrets of the Pros

"I will form good habits and become their slave."
—Og Mandino

If you have a room with windows, remember the following:

➤ Know where to find the rods and cords for the blinds.

➤ **Know how to open and close the windows.**

➤ **Arrange seating so that audience members have their backs to the window.**

➤ **Avoid rooms with many windows and no drapes.** Too much uncontrolled sun can kill a good presentation. It's bright, it's hot, and it moves, which means it will bother everyone in the room at some point in the day.

Room Seating

The seating arrangement for your room is critical. Don't leave your seating to chance or the evening set-up crew. You want to create an inviting, comfortable environment. This means audience members should have enough space to be comfortable and move freely. They should face you and be able to see each other as much as possible.

Three basic types of seating arrangements are used for medium-sized presentations:

1. **Classroom Style.** Audience members sit in groups of four or more at straight tables (or just in chairs). This style ensures the audience will see you and you will see them.

2. **Rounds.** Audience members sit clustered at round tables. Rounds create a feeling of camaraderie and encourage interaction.

3. **U-Shaped.** U-shape with the presenter situated in the middle allows flexibility.

Examples of seating arrangements can be found on page 165.

Sound Systems, Lighting, and Other Miscellany

What might seem small to you will often seem big to your audience. Busy as you are, you might overlook things like lighting, temperature, sound, and other factors that collectively contribute to audience comfort. The following guidelines will help you control audience comfort.

Sound System

If you intend to use music or other audiovisual media, you will be glad to know that many hotel seminar rooms and office buildings have built-in sound systems. I usually bring my own tape deck when I need audio support. However, if you do use on-site equipment, be sure to double-check the following:

➤ **Your equipment.** Save yourself the embarrassment of finding out that your equipment doesn't work in the middle of your presentation.

➤ **The location of volume controls, on/off switches, and other such things.** Always preset volume controls before your audience arrives.

➤ **Does sound carry to all parts of the room?** "Dead spots" can occur and distract people from your message.

Water/Refreshments

Whenever possible, keep refreshments on hand either inside or just outside of the room. This will prevent your group from scattering in search of sustenance every time you break. Make sure your group won't have to bottleneck at the coffee table, and see that there are enough refreshments on hand for everyone. It might not be your job, but it will be your face they are looking at when the coffee runs out. And always make sure you have a glass of water for yourself. It's difficult to speak effectively with a dry mouth.

Temperature

Temperature is the number-one environmental complaint during presentations. The following are a few tips for keeping your room comfortable and temperate for your audience members:

➤ **Know the name of the person who has the key.** If you're in one of those hotels or schoolrooms where the temperature controls are locked in a clear plastic box, make sure you know the person who has the key by name before your presentation starts. You'll be calling him or her at least once during the presentation.

Seating

LARGE GROUPS

0

| X X X X X X | X X X X X X |

X X X X X X   X X X X X X
X X X X X X   X X X X X X
X X X X X X   X X X X X X
X X X X X X   X X X X X X
X X X X X X   X X X X X X
X X X X X X   X X X X X X
X X X X X X   X X X X X X

MEDIUM-SIZED GROUPS

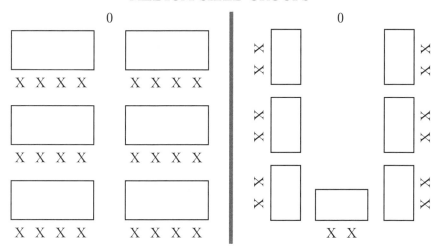

SMALL GROUPS

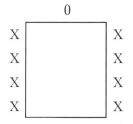

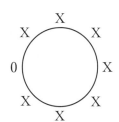

0 = Speaker

X = Audience Member

➤ **Arrive early and check the temperature.** When a room is unused for a day or more, heat gets turned off in the winter and air-conditioning gets turned off in the summer. Show up early enough to get your room back to the right temperature.

Electrical Outlets/Light Switches

You'll need both, so know where they are. The rule for lighting is this: full bright means high excitement. Keep the lights on as bright as possible throughout your presentation. If you must turn them down for projectors, turn off only a few or use dimmers. Always bring them back to full bright as soon as possible.

Visual Aids

Visual aids are the most common type of tool a presenter uses. Why? Because, next to you, they're the most effective vehicle for delivering your message and inspiring your presentation. To paraphrase Confucius: A visual aid is worth a thousand words.

Recent research supports what Confucius discovered ages ago. People understand a message better when words are reinforced by pictures. In fact, here's a thumbnail sketch of what we know about audiences and visual aids.

➤ **People receive information in different ways.**
- **Auditorially**—through the ears.
- **Kinetically**—through movement.
- **Visually**—through the eyes.

➤ **Most people tend to be visually oriented when it comes to learning.**

➤ **Good visual aids get a point across in three to five seconds.** Words take three to five minutes.

Good visual aids reinforce, clarify, and drive home points. They are indispensable for introducing or summarizing ideas, saving time, and helping the audience focus its attention. They also give *you* a break. While the audience is viewing a videotape, slide projection, or computer-generated presentation, their eyes are away from you, providing critical time to prepare the next section of your presentation, review your notes, or gather your thoughts.

When To Use Common Visual Aids

Any time you wish to emphasize a point — really drive it home — make sure the audience sees it in written form. Better yet, let them see it *drawn* out, as in a picture.

Visual aids should be used when you wish to accomplish the following:

➤ **Increase retention.**

➤ **Explain new concepts.**

➤ **Summarize new concepts.**

➤ **Present complex data such as statistics and graphs.**

➤ **Get the audience to look at something other than the speaker.**

➤ **Get the audience more involved.**

How To Use Common Visual Aids

The most common types of visual aids are the following:

➤ **Flip charts**

➤ **Handouts**

➤ **Overhead projectors**

➤ **Slide projectors**

➤ **Props**

➤ **Videotapes and films**

➤ **High-tech video equipment**

With visuals there is one golden rule: *Avoid the data dump.* Don't clutter the visual with information. The fewer words the better. Use pictures, and remember less is more. The following are *do's* and *don'ts* for using the most common visual aids:

➤ **Keep visuals simple.** Ideally, no more than five lines per page and five words per line should be written on anything the audience has to read. Graphs should be simple, clean, and easy to understand. Never clutter a screen or a page.

167

➤ **Keep visuals legible.** Write slowly and clearly. When possible, prepare everything on a computer or typewriter.

➤ **Keep visuals neat.** Written lines should be straight, graphs clear, and pictures centered.

➤ **Keep visuals consistent.** Your visual aids should be uniform and consistent in their appearance.

➤ **Keep visuals unified.** Each page or screen should address one topic or idea. If you move on to something else, start a clean visual.

➤ **Use bulleted points and sentence fragments (two- or three-word statements, usually without a verb) instead of full sentences.** Sentence fragments are easier for audiences to absorb.

➤ **Use pictures instead of sentence fragments, when possible.** Pictures are even easier to understand.

➤ **Combine pictures, symbols, and key words.**

➤ **Children's coloring books are a good source for pictures and drawings.** Use them to create overheads, pre-prepared flip charts, and handouts.

➤ **Make visuals colorful.**

➤ **Use graphics related to the subject matter.** This will help the audience retain key points.

Flip Charts

Flip charts are the most common visual aid. They're easy to use, effective, and relatively inexpensive. And that's not all that makes them great. I especially like the versatility of the flip chart. It's the "jeep" of the presentation world—it can go anywhere while you remian in control. When using a flip chart, you don't have to worry about finding an outlet, burning out a bulb, or dimming the lights. The following are the most common uses for flip charts:

➤ **Presenting information you wish to emphasize.**

➤ **Focusing audience attention in one place.**

➤ **Recording information—especially contributions from audience members.**

➤ Displaying what you've already covered.

➤ Encouraging audience involvement.

You should also be familiar with the *three* types of flip charts:

1. **The pre-drawn flip chart.** You prepare these flips before your audience arrives.

2. **The preplanned flip chart.** You plan these out and pencil in what you're going to write (audience members won't see the thin pencil marks), then trace over them in front of the audience.

3. **The "on-the-fly" flip chart**. You write these as you're moving along.

Most presenters have used flip charts at some time, but many have never bothered to learn how to use them correctly. Consider the following tips.

Hot Tips for Cool Flips

➤ **Use more than one flip chart, whenever possible.** Multiple flips give a feeling of energy and good planning.

➤ **Use only the top three-fourths of your flip chart.** Even those audience members sitting in the back can see everything you write.

➤ **Prepare as many flips as you can ahead of time.** They look better and are easier to read. When preparing flips, leave every other page blank to absorb any ink that bleeds through.

The Presentor (see p. 224)

True inspiration comes when your audience:

• Understands what you tell them

• Buys-in to the experience of listening to what you tell them

• Remembers what you tell them

Visual aids are valuable because they facilitate all three of these levels.

➤ **Use water-soluble markers rather than permanent ones.** This will keep the ink from staining your fingers.

➤ **Use scented markers.** They don't have the strong chemical smell of permanent markers.

➤ **Use a fat marker when printing.** Placing the flat end of a fat marker on the paper makes anyone's printing look good!

➤ **Use colors!** The more colorful the better.

➤ **Use darker colors.** You can see these better.

➤ **Draw a frame around the edge of the flip chart page for clarity.**

➤ **Use flip chart paper that has faint printed horizontal and vertical lines (graph paper).** This makes it easier for you to keep your lines straight.

➤ **Make sure every member of the audience can see the chart.**

➤ **Use an overhead to trace something on to a flip chart when you're preparing it.**

➤ **Post finished flips on the walls.** This shows your audience how much material you're covering and "decorates" the room with a record of the presentation.

➤ **Number your flip charts as you put them on the wall.**

➤ **Have pre-torn strips of masking tape ready for posting the flips on the wall.** You can stick the strips on the back of the flip chart stand *before* your presentation begins.

➤ **Tear off only one sheet at a time.**

➤ **When taking dictation from your audience, do your best to use their exact words.** This makes audience members feel like pros.

➤ **Have extra markers of all sizes and colors.**

➤ **Consider the distance from your chart to the back row.** If the back row would have trouble seeing, use an overhead.

➤ **Use prepared flips to keep yourself on track.**

➤ **Solicit volunteer "scribes" from the audience to help you write on flip charts.** Audience members will enjoy the attention, and you won't have to write while you speak.

The only real drawback to flip charts is their size. If the room or audience is too large, people near the back will have a difficult time seeing what you've written. For this reason, flip charts are best for small- to medium-sized groups (fewer than 100 people).

Overheads and Slides

Overheads, slides, and computer presentations work well for larger groups because they can be seen from everywhere in the room. Two of these presentation formats are familiar to us in other settings: the overhead projector from school, and the slide-show from our parents' vacation slides.

Computer-generated presentations are the latest technology and the wave of the future. In addition, computer-generated graphics reduce the need to darken the room to enhance viewing and allow the presenter to move freely about the room using a laser pointer and a remote mouse to advance and highlight the material.

While computers represent the latest technology, some presenters will be unable to afford these tools and will stay with overheads and slides. Whatever tools you choose, always test your overheads, slides, or computer presentation well before the audience arrives.

Consider the following tips when using overheads, slides, and computer presentations:

➤ **Overheads should support your presentation, not replace it.**

➤ **Use the 5x5 rule.** Aim for no more than five points and five words per point on each transparency.

➤ **When using an overhead, also use a pointer.**

➤ **Don't hold the pointer on the screen.** It will shake and make you look nervous. Instead, move the pointer in a circular motion.

➤ **Use sleeves to keep transparencies neat.**

➤ **Put notes in the margins if you use sleeves.**

➤ **Don't leave an "empty" white-light screen while you're talking.** It's distracting to audience members.

➤ **Create a cardboard "light-hood" to turn overheads on and off.**

➤ **Check for typos!** They stand out in an overhead.

➤ When revealing steps, consider using overlays instead of cover-ups.

➤ Always carry a spare bulb; sooner or later you'll need it.

➤ Carry a few blank transparencies.

➤ Whenever possible, place the screen right or left of the center of the room. Center stage belongs to the speaker.

➤ Always number your overheads in case they're dropped.

➤ If speaking about an overhead slide, move in front of the overhead projector, not through the light.

➤ Use overhead markers to draw lines and circle key words to focus the presentation.

➤ Become familiar with mouse sensitivity by practicing extensively by yourself.

➤ If you are relying on another person's computer equipment for support, establish compatability of the systems well in advance.

➤ Be sure you know how to connect your computer to visual display devices (TV sets, monitors, video projection devices).

➤ Carry a backup set of overheads or slides in the event the computer presentation encounters technical problems.

Handouts

Handouts—those sheets of paper you give to audience members periodically throughout the day—are useful for a number of reasons. They give audience members a feeling of partial ownership in your presentation, and they are about as versatile as flip charts but can hold more information. If time and budget allow, always use handouts!

➤ Consider handouts for the following:

- Statistics
- Graphs
- Examples
- Comparisons

- Quotations
- Expert testimonials

➤ **Handouts should match the sequence of the talk.**

➤ **Distribute handouts at the right time.** Too early or too late can confuse the audience.

➤ **When developing handouts, ask yourself, "What information will people really want to take with them?"**

➤ **Consider what the audience will actually *do* with the handout.**

➤ **Keep handouts to a minimum to ensure they are properly valued by the audience.**

➤ **Use handouts that tie in with your other visuals, when possible.**

➤ **Make sure your handouts have space for note taking, when possible.**

➤ **Use graphics and bulleted points.** Avoid expository passages of text unless the handout is an essential reprint of a definitive article or story.

➤ **Consider a summary handout.**

➤ **Number the pages so the audience can follow along.**

➤ **Keep handouts simple and clear — neatness counts.**

➤ **Always prepare extra handouts.**

➤ **Hole punch handouts.**

➤ **Consider making handouts the size your audience members can put into binders, Daytimers, Franklin Planners, or other places where they keep important information.**

➤ **Organize all handouts ahead of time for quick distribution.**

➤ **If appropriate, ask audience volunteers to help distribute handouts.** Reward them at the end of the presentation with applause or a small prize.

Secrets of the Pros

"If using multiple handouts, use different color paper for each one. Easier to refer to or back to (i.e., 'Let's look at the blue handout')."
—Alan Jones

Videos

For the most part, videos have replaced the film projector in the presentation business. Sophisticated motion pictures can be developed at a relatively low cost. Videos are also good for recording previous presentations, testimonials, and other scenarios that might interest your audience. The biggest drawback to videos is that unless you have a large screen, they can be hard to see — especially text. If you have an audience of more than 25, you'll need two TV screens, one for each side of the room. That can be expensive and cumbersome.

In any case, if you wish to use video, you'll need a video cassette recorder (VCR) and a monitor or television for your presentations. You'll also need a video cart or a tall table on which to place them. Presenters can rent equipment or use their own. Video is a powerful aid, and one well worth mastering. Study the following tips:

➤ **Check video equipment well in advance.** A small problem detected early can save you embarrassment and time in the middle of your presentation.

➤ **Preset volume levels.** Sit in the last row and determine how well you can hear.

➤ **Check picture quality the same way.**

➤ **Cue your videotapes before using them.**

➤ **If you're making your own videotapes, leave space between segments so you can cue them.**

➤ **Avoid surprises.** If someone else is making the videotape, be sure you memorize or write out the sequence.

➤ **Always carry a spare tape.**

➤ **Always carry spare cables.**

Props

Props are three-dimensional visual aids. They are "the actual thing" you're talking about or a model of it. Props work best when you're talking about complicated subjects that audience members actually need to see and feel. They're also entertaining.

The biggest drawback with props is that you have to cart them around wherever you go, and they can be expensive to create and replace. Consider the following tips:

➤ **Be creative.** Use common items that anyone can get their hands on. Your imagination can help you save money.

➤ **Be sure to display the prop long enough for everyone to get a good look.**

➤ **Pass the prop around, if possible.**

➤ **Prepare duplicate props.**

➤ **Keep props in a bag or box to heighten excitement, then "reveal" them.**

Twenty-First Century Presentations

Every day, new presentation tools are developed. The following are some of the technologies available to you:

➤ **CDI.** That's short for Compact Disk Interactive equipment. Like a VCR or CD, CDI gives the presenter mobility, a great picture, and most importantly, a level of interactivity and presentation flexibility previously unheard of.

➤ **Presentation software.** Companies are producing new softwares regularly. Pop the program in your computer and you have terrific-looking visuals you can shine on a screen.

➤ **Laptop computers.** These lightweight, powerful devices now process data at speeds equal to your "big computer." Utilizing these machines in presentations allows you to combine video, graphics, and even audio into an integrated, powerful, multi-media experience. Although cost is a factor and the technical challenges can be significant, results can be incredible when properly coordinated.

Toolbox

Some tools are so important that a presenter should *never* leave home without them. I carry these in a rolling airport suitcase that serves as a traveling office and presentations center. You'll want to develop your own system. I urge you to include all of the tools on the following page in your presenter's toolbox:

➤ **Pointer.** There are wooden pointers, retractable pointers that look like pens and extend like car antennas, and laser pointers that project a little red dot wherever you aim them.

➤ **Colored magic markers (scented).**

➤ **Scissors.**

➤ **Extension cords.**

➤ **Camera.** Polaroids work best. You can take pictures of activities, then give them away to audience members as freebies.

➤ **Tape.**

• **Masking tape for flips.**

• **Transparent tape for handouts and miscellaneous uses.**

• **Surgical tape.** It works as whiteout for your flip charts and is very strong.

➤ **Push pins.** Tape won't stick to cloth-covered walls. Use push pins for hanging flip charts.

➤ **An assortment of markers, pens, pencils, and scratch pads.**

➤ **Breath mints.** You'll be glad you took them.

➤ **Whistle.** This is for high-energy fun.

➤ **Stopwatch.** This is for keeping yourself on schedule and timing business entertainment activities.

➤ **Overhead markers.** Use the type you can wipe off from transparencies.

➤ **Aspirin.** Don't try to deal with headaches while presenting!

One Last Note

I've gone over many of the tools and aids you can use in your presentation, but don't let all this information overwhelm you. Select the tools that are right for your presentation and your personality.

Always remember that practice makes perfect—the more you use the tools, the more comfortable you'll become. Rehearse with the props, flip charts, overheads, and other tools that you'll use on presentation day. The tools are there to make your job easier, not more difficult, and increase your audience's enjoyment and retention. Use them accordingly, and you'll be on your way to mastering the powerful tools of the presentation trade.

Very Important Points To Remember

✔ The room is a tool. Become as familiar with your room as you are with all your other tools.

✔ Statistics show that we remember 20 percent of what we hear, 30 percent of what we see, and 50 percent of what we see *and* hear. Use visual aids!

✔ Visual aids:

➤ **Increase retention**

➤ **Explain new concepts**

➤ **Summarize new concepts**

➤ **Present complex data such as statistics and graphs**

➤ **Get the audience to look at something other than the speaker**

➤ **Get the audience more involved**

✔ Check and double-check your tools. A little problem can become a big problem if you don't notice it until you're in the middle of your presentation.

✔ Know how to use the most common types of visual aids:

➤ **Flip charts**

➤ **Handouts**

➤ **Overhead projectors**

➤ **Slide projectors**

➤ **Props**

➤ **Videotapes**

✔ Develop an effective presenter's toolbox that works for you. Then don't leave home without it!

Fill in Your Favorite Tips from the Chapter

✔ _____

_____

✔ _____

_____

This chapter reveals:

➤ How to manage your presentation

➤ How to ask for and use feedback from your audience

➤ How to handle questions and answers

10

Managing Your Presentation

"Your listeners won't care how much you know until they know how much you care."

— Anonymous

The Scene...

Your presentation seems to be going smoothly — no one has fallen asleep, no one has gotten up to leave, but you'd like to be sure things are working. Occasionally throughout the presentation, you ask the audience whether they have questions. You get some shaking heads, a few shrugs, and a lot of silence. It could mean that you're doing such a good job that they understand everything — or it could mean they're totally lost. What you need is a simple system for

Secrets of the Pros
"Say 'thank you' many times."
— Dottie Walters

179

polling your audience to find out how the presentation is working and how to manage it better for them.

The Solution . . .

Learn to use *verbal surveying* and *targeted polling* to obtain honest, usable audience feedback. Audiences are full of information that will help you manage your presentation. Make sure you take advantage of it!

Secrets

1. **Make sure there is a continual buildup of excitement from section to section.** Learn to use Business Entertainment™.

2. **Use transitions between the sections of your presentation.**

   ➤ **Introduce new material.**

   ➤ **Sum up before moving on.**

3. **Always give clear and simple directions.**

4. **Use *verbal surveying* to get feedback from the group.**

5. **Use *targeted polling* to get feedback from individuals.**

6. **Know how to handle questions, and answer effectively.**

Managing Your Presentations

Managing your presentation means mastering the mechanics of moving from section to section. A presentation is not one long, uninterrupted talk, but rather, a group of related subsections, strung together to present ideas and concepts to your audience.

So far we've primarily dealt with how to develop, rehearse, and present those sections that make up your presentation. But making a smooth transition requires another skill—you have to be a good administrator. Unfortunately, many presenters neglect this important element. It requires the following management skills:

➤ **The ability to give clear, concise directions**

➤ **The ability to be decisive**

➤ The ability to stick to a schedule

➤ The ability to remain flexible

➤ The ability to solicit and apply feedback from your audience

Audience Members

In order to ensure that your audience is maintaining interest and retaining information, they must be continually monitored. *Verbal surveying* and *targeted polling* are methods for gathering and interpreting audience response as the presentation moves along.

Rather than trying to survey the entire audience, pick two or three faces from the group and make these folks your audience barometers throughout the day. In chapter 2, I discussed *four* basic types of audience members: Prisoners, Vacationers, Graduates, and Students. Try to find a face from at least two of these groups. Note their attitudes at the beginning of the presentation, during the body of your presentation, and at the beginning of the first activity. Ask yourself the following questions:

➤ **What was the attitude of the audience member when he or she arrived?**

➤ **What was the attitude of the audience member when I began to speak?**

➤ **How has the audience member's attitude changed?**

Don't deliver your presentation to these people exclusively. You'll still want to concentrate on the entire room, but by monitoring two or three faces consistently, you'll have a rough idea how your presentation is going.

Transitions

I mention transitions in this chapter because transitions are more than just the words or phrases you use to glue together different sections of your presentation. Transitions *do* glue the end of one section to the beginning of the next and provide a natural flow from one key point to another. But their most important job is to build interest.

181

Transitions Build Audience Interest

Transitions build bridges between your presentation's key points. Many presenters spend hours and hours developing their presentations. More hours rehearsing, and even more hours getting the room ready. Then they negate all their work by failing to carefully build in and use transitions.

Listening is hard work and the quickest way to lose track of an audience is by failing to tell them where you're going. This is a big mistake! Audience members need signals and guideposts, just like travelers, to reassure them that they are on the right track and that it's worth their effort to continue down this road. Transitions in your presentation provide these mental guideposts.

The general rule for transitions is this: Use one whenever you move from one major idea to another. It tells your audience that you've summed up "idea one" and you're moving to "idea two."

It doesn't take a lot of words—usually a sentence or two will do. But the one problem many of the presenters I've coached and trained consistently exhibit is forgetting to use transitions *at all*. It's an easy mistake to make in the excitement of the presentation.

Bored faces are not necessarily a sign that you and your presentation are boring. Often it's just that your audience doesn't know where you are headed. Relate the core of your talk back to them by obeying the following rules on transitions:

➤ **Use transitions between all important ideas you present.**

➤ **Use transitions to introduce and sum up new ideas, activities, or even before taking a break.**

➤ **Keep transitions short and sweet.** They are the mortar, not the bricks, of your presentation.

➤ **Use attention-getting statements, relative statistics, and humor.**

➤ **Vary your transitions.**

➤ **Use gestures and body movements.**

Examples of transitions are as follows:

➤ **"This sums up what we need to understand about A; now let's look at B."**

➤ **"In the next hour, I plan to show you X, Y, and Z."**

➤ **"Not only do these numbers show the problem, if we look at them closely, they reveal the solution."**

Use your imagination, and remember, transitions keep your audience interested, join each one of your ideas to another, and, most importantly, provide your audience with important guideposts to keep them on track. Use them!

Giving Directions

Closely related to providing transitions is giving directions. Again, directions serve as guideposts to your audience and cut down on confusion. Your audience will be feeling the following *four* tensions:

Secrets of the Pros

"Too many people try to put too much information in one presentation, a big mistake; keep it simple."

—Dale Ware

1. **Tension between audience members**

2. **Tension between audience members and you, the presenter**

3. **Tension between audience members and the materials you've given them**

4. **Tension between audience members and their environment**

Audience members feel these tensions because they are unsure of what to expect. (See chapter 4.)

Whenever you ask your audience to do something—even if it is simply to jot down an idea or take a break—give them a clear idea of what to do. Audience members don't know what you want unless you tell them, and they don't know your personality. Will the presenter embarrass them if they make a mistake or come back late? Confusion is a close cousin to boredom—and both are deadly to your presentation. Whenever you set up an activity or ask the audience to do something, invest in the two minutes it takes to give clear instructions.

Remember the following guidelines for instructing your audience:

➤ **Plan ahead.** Instructions for activities, breaks, using materials, or anything else requiring audience participation should be planned out in advance.

➤ **Break your instructions into clear, briefly defined steps.**

➤ **Try to keep these points to a small number.** Anything more than five steps will confuse the audience.

➤ **When you arrive at the point in your presentation where instructions are needed, announce to the audience, "I have a few simple steps for doing this activity."**

➤ **Write the steps out in brief, bulleted points on a flip chart.** Audience members can look up to make sure they're on the right track.

➤ **Be prepared to answer questions about your instructions.**

A little time spent giving clear instructions will save a lot of time later unraveling confusion and getting your audience back on track. Your presentation will run more smoothly and your ideas and activities will become much more effective when your audience knows exactly what you want.

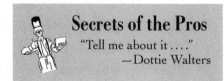

Secrets of the Pros
"Tell me about it . . . ."
—Dottie Walters

The Audience: Verbal Surveying

Verbal surveying is a method used to ensure that the entire room is benefiting from the presentation. Audiences rarely complain, which often means they are quietly putting up with something that is annoying them, distracting them, or otherwise occupying their attention and hurting your presentation.

Rather than passively waiting for the audience to give you information on things like room temperature, the pace of your presentation, or even the difficulty of the content, become proactive by verbally surveying the room. Also take advantage of breaks and activity time to ask quality-control questions of random audience members. The following, for example:

➤ **Are you comfortable?** Too hot—too cold? Can you hear and see clearly?

➤ **How would you rate the quality of my content?**

➤ **Is the pace of my presentation too slow or too fast?**

➤ **Are you being entertained?**

➤ **Are you retaining the material I'm presenting?**

If audience members admit something isn't going correctly, fix it! Otherwise you've wasted your time and hurt your credibility. Above all, don't take criticism personally. View it as an opportunity to make your presentation even better!

Individuals: "Targeted Polling"

Targeted polling is similar to *verbal surveying,* except you select a few individuals and ask them questions throughout the presentation. Select two or three individuals from the group very near the beginning. Keep an eye on how they respond to your material, occasionally asking them specific questions about specific sections. Choosing a few people to monitor the course of the presentation will give you an idea how your presentation is developing for each audience member.

You can really take advantage of one-on-one *targeted polling* during breaks and/or lunch time. Choose an audience member and talk with him or her during the break. Ask for suggestions. Audience members love the one-on-one attention and often become champions for the presenter.

What's in It for Me?

The most important thing you can do to manage your presentation and make sure it runs smoothly is to put yourself in your audience's shoes and continually ask yourself, "What's in it for me?"

Every audience member needs a reason to listen to what you are saying. It's not enough to explain what some concept, idea, behavior, product, or anything else *is* or how it works. To interest an audience, you have to drive your message home by telling them *what it does for them.*

From the moment you begin designing your presentation to the moment you close it, be aware of the reasons your audience will have to listen. Continually relate your talk to these. Everyone wants something. The following are good motivators:

> **Secrets of the Pros**
>
> "We all have a story to tell, and people want to hear that story. Tell your story well, with a high level of energy, and you will always have an audience willing to listen."
>
> —Frank Walker

➤ **Material gain**

➤ **Fame**

➤ **Respect**

➤ **Glory**

➤ **Prestige**

➤ **Self-advancement**

➤ **Approval**

➤ **Peace of mind**

Make sure you're delivering something your audience needs and wants. Do it well and regularly, and your audience will respond.

Work the Whole Room

During your presentation, work the *entire* room. That means making sure every audience member feels involved and has reason to continue listening to you.

> Make your presentation meaningful to the audience by getting your audience physically involved and tie all key points to their needs. All audiences are asking this question: what's in it for me? A skydiver will not become bored learning to pack her own parachute. Her reward for learning the skill is too important.
>
> —**Myra Ketterman**

You can maintain contact with the whole room by:

➤ **Moving.** Don't stand in one place.

➤ **Maintaining eye contact.** Look everyone in the eye for a few moments on a regular basis.

➤ **Walking into your audience.** Don't stand behind a podium or lectern if you can help it. Move through the audience.

I also ask people to smile when we start. For example, when I ask someone to write something down, I then ask the individual to look at me *and smile* when he or she is finished. I acknowledge each as they look up. It's important to maintain eye contact with everyone in the room, and let them drive the activity. Work the room!

Answering Questions: How To Avoid Getting Tripped Up

The question of questions—when to ask for them and how to answer them—is an issue we'll address more fully a little later. However, questions at the early stage of a presentation—that point when you're letting the audience in on your objectives and getting them to buy-in to the day—raise special issues. At this stage of the game there will be *three* basic kinds of questions:

1. **What-does-it-all-mean** questions. These require a long-winded answer which you don't want to provide this early in your presentation.

2. **When-will-we . . .** questions. These should be answered within the normal course of the presentation.

3. **Who-do-you-think-you-are** questions. These questions are often hostile. The intent is to test your authority.

Although the first two are a little easier than the third, in general, all these types of questions must be dealt with swiftly.

Type 1 questions require a *parent's* skill and can usually be answered with a simple, "That's a question we don't have time to answer right now, but we'll discuss where you might find the answer during our break."

Type 2 questions require a *teacher's* skill. "We'll be covering that topic in a few minutes," will usually do.

Type 3 questions require the subtle, tough skills of a *coach*. The trick is to: a) rephrase the question in your own words, and b) provide an answer that avoids arrogance and keeps you looking dignified. For example, someone might ask, "What's the value of my being here?" Your answer might be, "We're going to cover some points that are designed to make your life a little easier, and we might even have some fun doing it." Neutralizing negative questions can be a great way to prove yourself.

In general, there are *three* basic mistakes presenters make when unexpected questions are asked:

1. **Answering too soon**

2. **Answering too much**

3. **Creating a pointless dialogue with one person**

The key is to expect the unexpected question. This doesn't mean knowing what the question will be, but having a ready method for answering any question. The following tips will help you prepare:

➤ **Brainstorm possible questions during your preparation.**

➤ **Write out these questions and their answers on a 3x5 card.**

➤ **Practice responding to questions with an associate.**

➤ **When an audience member asks a question, always repeat the question to make sure everyone hears it.** This makes the audience member feel as if the question was intelligent and gives you time to think.

➤ **Listen to the whole question.** Don't interrupt a question, don't make fun of a question, and never finish a question from an audience member.

➤ **Involve the whole audience with your answer.** Ask for audience members to provide input.

➤ **Don't get stuck in a dialogue that will bore the audience member.** Tell the questioner you'll see him during a break or after the talk.

➤ **When someone asks a question, make sure you understand the question before answering.**

➤ **For confusing questions, get a better understanding of the question by asking for clarification.** Don't try to answer a question you don't fully understand.

➤ **Facilitate the questioning.** Bounce questions back to the audience to get them thinking.

➤ **Pause a moment when someone asks you a question.** This makes you look serious and gives you time to think.

➤ **Learn the art of bridging.** Refocus the question in a way that connects the listener's question with the point you're trying to make.

➤ **Don't guess if you don't know.**

➤ **Don't allow one or two audience members to dominate the questioning.**

➤ **Give answers everyone can understand.**

➤ **Practice and rehearse your answers.**

➤ **Always address the questions.** You don't have to know all the answers but you do have to acknowledge all the questions.

➤ **Anticipate and rehearse possible questions prior to the presentation.**

➤ **Never close your presentation with a question-and-answer period.** It can raise doubts and undo your presentation. Take questions long before you close.

Questions are your chance to show the audience your knowledge *and* your honesty. Don't fake an answer. The willingness to help find the *correct* answer will impress the audience more than the willingness to give any answer, even an incorrect one.

Very Important Points To Remember

✔ Managing your audience means seeing things from their point of view. Strive to make your presentation work for them.

✔ A confused audience is difficult to manage. Always sum up and use transitions before moving on to keep audience members aware of where the presentation is going.

✔ Whenever you ask the audience to do something, make sure you give clear instructions. Write the instructions on a flip chart so audience members can refer back to them.

✔ To get feedback and gauge your audience's response to your presentation, use *verbal surveying* and *targeted polling*.

✔ Know how to answer questions; the skilled handling of questions builds audience trust.

Fill in Your Favorite Tips from the Chapter

✔ _____
_____
_____

✔ _____
_____
_____

✔ _____
_____
_____

✔ _____
_____
_____

✔ _____
_____

PART 4
Closing Your Presentation

This chapter reveals:

➤ The difference between summarizing and closing

➤ How and why to summarize throughout the day

➤ How to use summarizing to set up a terrific ending

11

Summarizing

JEARY THEORY

Summarizing appeals to your audience's rational faculty. I always confirm value!

"It's what you learn after you know it all that counts."
— John Wooden

The Scene...

Your presentation has been a full day long. You've covered a ton of material and you need to make sure your audience takes away a few very important points to ensure that your words become action—but how?

The Solution...

Part of the Jeary Theory for giving presentations is that you should get the audience to tell you what you're going to tell them, let them tell you what you're telling them (verbal surveying and targeted polling) and finally, get them to tell you what you've told them. Summarizing effectively allows you to accomplish that third and most important step — driving your information home.

193

Secrets

1. Summarize throughout the day.
2. As you conclude your presentation, link the closing to the introduction.
3. Before beginning your close, summarize all the main points and tie the presentation together.
4. Prove you've met your objectives and those you set for your audience.
5. Give your audience closure even before you conclude.
6. Focus the presentation.
7. Keep it short.

Summarize Throughout the Day

Many presenters fail to create clear, effective summaries. This mistake is easy to make. After all, you understand the information you're presenting very well and now you're interested in moving swiftly from point to point. Isn't that better than slowing down and boring your audience members by rehashing what's already been covered? The answer is a resounding NO! You will not bore your audience by summarizing points. You will, however, accomplish *three* important things:

1. **You'll keep your audience focused.** Letting them know where they've been is the best way to let them know where they're heading.

2. **You'll increase your audience's retention rate.** A good way to set the points of your presentation in the minds of your audience members is by summarizing exactly what's important about what you've told them.

3. **You'll heighten the audience's interest by reducing confusion.**

The key to effective summarizing at the *close* of your presentation is to summarize *throughout the day*. Each time you conclude an activity or a segment of your presentation that includes a key point, make sure you summarize it for the audience. Use the following formula:

1. Introduce the key point.
2. Explain it.
3. Discuss it and engage in activities.
4. Recap the key point.
5. Provide a transition.
6. Introduce the new key point.

Once you establish this dynamic, the audience will find it easy to follow you, and they'll trust what you have to say. When you summarize, be sure to do the following:

➤ Always signal the audience that you are summarizing points.

➤ Ask them what they think the main points are—they'll retain what they say better than if they hear you say it.

➤ Write their answers on a flip chart.

➤ Add any point that your audience doesn't include.

When summarizing, keep it short, simple, and clear. Your summaries should last *no more than one or two minutes*. Know ahead of time what three points will sum up any of your key ideas, statements, etc. An audience receives a blizzard of information, even in the shortest presentation. Summarizing helps them understand what's really important!

Summarizing throughout the presentation has an added benefit. It gives you and your audience the practice you'll need to summarize just before you close the presentation. Continuous summarization prepares the audience intellectually *and* emotionally for the close. Remember, there's a difference between closing and summarizing:

➤ **Summarizing** drives your points home intellectually for the audience. It also prepares them emotionally for your close.

➤ **Closing** allows you to emotionally motivate your audience to act on everything that has come before.

The End of Your Presentation

Audience members, like all other people, usually think with their rational minds, but act on emotion. While it is important to motivate

195

your audience emotionally at the end of the presentation, you still can't skip the rational, intellectual part. This is what summarizing at the end of your presentation does.

Too often, even experienced presenters want to rush from their last major point into a big, emotional close. But doing so leaves out a crucial step—the summary. Unless you remember to summarize the main points from your presentation, your audience will lack closure and will not be fully inspired to *act* on your words.

When you come to the end of your presentation material, take a moment to reiterate your opening statement. This will link the end of the presentation to your earlier points and begin the process of closure for your audience.

Very Important Points

You'll notice that at the end of each chapter, I've included "Very Important Points to Remember." I have also used the VIP concept in major training initiatives. A few years ago, I realized that almost every presentation has too many points for an audience to remember. If you don't provide closure point by point or wrap up the presentation by providing the closure a summary delivers, your audience won't know what to take with them.

To solve the problem, I use the VIP method. Audience members in many of my seminars receive a booklet called a "VIP note taker," in which *they* can write down the points they find most important. At the end of each segment, I ask for a few examples of important points from audience members. Not only does this engage them, it also creates audience buy-in because *they* are in control of what is important. The VIP method:

➤ **Increases retention**

➤ **Increases audience buy-in**

➤ **Puts audience members in charge**

➤ **Makes audience members the heroes**

Try the VIP method next time *you* give a presentation!

The opening and closing are the most important parts of your presentation. When summing up at the end of the day, remind your audience of the opening and prepare them for the close. Just as meeting and greeting is a critical setup for your opening, so effective summarizing is the critical setup for your close. It ties the presentation together and prepares your audience emotionally.

Prove You've Met Your Objectives and Your Audience's Expectations

Once you've tied the end to the beginning, the next step is to prove you've met your objectives. By reviewing these objectives, you give the audience a clear idea of what you've done. At this stage, you will also want to review the main points of your presentation. Prepare handouts or an overhead for doing so. This will create a sort of "high-points" review for the audience.

At the beginning, you asked your audience for their expectations and wrote them down on a flip chart. Now it is time for the payoff. Return your audience's attention to the flip chart and go over their expectations, one by one, remembering that you have met or exceeded each one. Since your audience helped create the list, you will already have them on your side. They'll see in seconds that you delivered what you promised.

Focus the Presentation

Your summary should bring all the various ideas and images of your presentation into sharp focus. The following are the basic steps to delivering an effective summary:

1. **Let your audience know you are summarizing the points of the presentation.** Ask what they believe were the major points.

2. **Review your objectives from the opening.** It's good to let them know you achieved them.

3. **Review their expectations from the beginning of the presentation as well.**

4. **Keep your summary short. It should take no more than five minutes.** Anything longer will begin to seem redundant and unnecessary.

Summarizing

197

5. Include your audience. If they say it was important—it was!

Remember, your audience needs closure before they move into the real closing. Deliver this by taking a few minutes to sum up the presentation.

Very Important Points To Remember

✔ Summarizing and closing are two different things.

✔ Summarizing ties the themes of the presentation together and creates intellectual buy-in for audience members.

✔ Closing creates emotional *buy-in* and inspires the audience to *act on* your words.

✔ Effective summarizing means tying the end of your presentation to the beginning of your presentation.

✔ Effective summarizing means proving you've met your objectives *and* the audience's expectations.

✔ Effective summarizing means clearly reviewing the most important concepts of the day and what they mean for your audience.

✔ An effective summary provides closure for the presentation's information and sets up a powerful closing.

Fill in Your Favorite Tips from the Chapter

✔ _____

_____

✔ _____

_____

✔ _____

_____

✔ _____

_____

✔ _____

_____

✔ _____

_____

✔ _____

_____

✔ _____

_____

✔ _____

_____

✔ _____

_____

✔ _____

_____

✔ _____

_____

This chapter reveals:

➤ How to close after you've summarized

➤ How to use emotion to ensure audience buy-in

➤ What to avoid when closing

12

Close It Right!

JEARY THEORY ━━━━━━━━━━

A fine closing will make your audience feel good about what they've learned, inspire them to act, and leave them with something by which to remember you and your key message.

"Great is the art of beginning; but greater is the art of ending."

—Henry Wadsworth Longfellow

Secrets

1. Use emotion in your close.

2. Always include a call to action.

3. Try to invoke a future challenge.

4. Go over the next steps.

5. Closing killers:

➤ Q&A

➤ Apologizing

➤ Admitting you missed something

➤ Skipping the summary

➤ Rambling on

Saying Good-bye

Your presentation should end with a bang! The best openings are attention-grabbers. The same is true of closes, so many of the same techniques can be used. Some, of course, will be more appropriate than others, but all of them should solidify the common ground you've been covering from the beginning of your presentation.

The following are a few good attention-grabbers:

➤ **Questions that challenge participants and leave them pondering a course of action**

➤ **Quotations that form the basis for a rhetorical closing question**

➤ **A personal anecdote that illustrates the points made in the talk**

➤ **A slice-of-life story that illustrates the ending of your presentation**

➤ **An analogy that brings the main points of your presentation together**

These "attention-grabbers" function as transitions to prepare the audience to leave your presentation. Once you've gotten their attention, give them a reason for believing the words they've heard and, more importantly, inspire them to act on those words.

Appeal to Emotion

Closing is much more than merely bringing your presentation to an end. The close is the last—and luckily the most powerful—opportunity to inspire your audience. Think of summarizing and closing as a one-two punch. In the summary, you've set the stage by reaffirming value to the audience and setting them up for the emotional punch of the close.

By emotion I mean that you should appeal to what is human in your audience. Just like any great symphony or play, the final stanza of a presentation should tie together all that led to the end and then deliver an emotional

Secrets of the Pros

"I always try to recap by restating the points just reviewed and then leaving the audience with a single challenge that everyone can buy into."
—Paul Boitmann

punch. By this stage of the presentation, you should have covered everything that appeals to the audience's rational mind. Now it's time to appeal to emotion and get them to act.

The following are basic rules for any close:

➤ **Appeal to emotion.** Your audience thinks with their rational minds but acts on emotion.

➤ **Keep it short.** The close itself should last no more than two minutes. If you take any longer, the emotional power will turn syrupy.

➤ **Be positive.** Never discuss negatives.

➤ **Be motivational.** Assure your audience that their actions do matter.

➤ **Be energetic.** Your energy and enthusiasm will inspire the audience more than anything you have to say. If the last thing they see is your enthusiasm, they will leave feeling enthusiastic and ready to act.

Prepare Your Ending

It's a good idea to have a clear picture of your close before you get there. The worst ending is one that simply goes: "Well, I guess that's about it, any questions?" You can avoid this poor ending by knowing what you will say at the end and saying it with emotion. To determine what direction your close should take, ask yourself the following questions:

➤ **What does my audience want?**

➤ What objections will my audience have that might keep them from putting my message into action?

➤ How strong a case have I made?

➤ What are the next steps my audience must take to act on my presentation?

An appeal to your audience's emotions requires that you be on common emotional ground since your appeal relies upon the assumption of common beliefs and feelings. This is true for even the stuffiest audiences. The chairman of a company fighting a takeover bid, for example, may call on company loyalty and history to urge stockholders to reject the tendered offer. Emotion is always *appropriate, provided you consider the type of audience you have and what their needs are.*

That Warm and Fuzzy Feeling

The close is literally your last word to the audience. Make the most of it by keeping it short and making sure it's something that will inspire the audience to act. Consider using the following:

> Appealing to his audience to speak out in defense of their beliefs, Washington state's licensing director, R. Y. Woodhouse, closed with a story told by a minister during the Holocaust:
>
> > ". . . They came first for the Communists, and I didn't speak up because I wasn't a Communist.
> >
> > "Then they came for the Jews, and I didn't speak up because I wasn't a Jew.
> >
> > "Then they came for the trade unionists, and I didn't speak up because I wasn't a trade unionist.
> >
> > "Then they came for the Catholics, and I didn't speak up because I was a Protestant.
> >
> > "Then they came for me, and by that time no one was left to speak."
>
> His appeal was largely emotional. But it was also dignified and, in the end, extremely powerful.

1. **Quotations** on almost any subject can be found in sourcebooks for speakers.

2. **Stories** are good when you need to make a point and drive it home with emotion. The following types of stories are especially effective:

   ➤ **Success stories**

   ➤ **Rags-to-riches stories**

   ➤ **Depression-to-elation stories**

   ➤ **Defeat-to-victory stories**

3. **Calls to action** remind the audience that words only matter when they lead to action. They are an emotionally effective and satisfying way to end your presentation—for them and for you.

4. **Next steps** are those things audience members can do to actually put words into actions that will benefit them. Be sure to cover these with your audience.

Closing Killers

Avoid the following at all costs:

➤ **Asking for questions at the end of your presentation.** This is the single most common—and unfortunately most devastating—way to close. It moves the audience's focus from your message, introduces doubts, and lasts for an indefinite length of time. The right place to solicit questions is just before you go into your summary. (See chapter 11.)

➤ **Apologizing.** Don't apologize at all, but if you must, never do it at the end.

➤ **Admitting something was missed.** It's too late to go back so why admit you missed something? Move on.

➤ **Skipping the summary.** This leaves the audience dangling and instead of ending with a warm, fuzzy feeling, you get only the fuzzy.

➤ **Rambling.** Your close should be short and sweet. Anything longer than two minutes will become sappy.

Close It Right!

The Send-Off

Always include a farewell in your close, and make it as enthusiastic as your welcome. Often, your audience will applaud. Accept it graciously and with a smile. Audiences have a need to give applause—who are you to stop them? Make sure you do *three* things at the end of your presentation:

1. **Thank the audience for their time and participation.**

2. **Say good-bye!**

3. **Remain available until all audience members have left.**

> ### Secrets of the Pros
>
> "My experience with people is that they generally do what you expect them to do."
> —Mary Kay Ash, founder Mary Kay Cosmetics

This last point is very important and often overlooked. Never deny your audience members an opportunity to speak to you after your talk. Remain as enthusiastic as you were throughout the presentation. Many a presenter has succeeded in creating a terrific presentation and a perfect close only to undo it all by failing to be accessible to the audience afterward. Allow your audience to speak with you, ask questions, and thank you after you're done. You are on stage until you're back at home!

Congratulations!

You have reached the end of your presentation—and almost the end of the book. Follow the advice, study the concepts, use it as a handy reference guide, and your skills as a presenter will increase. In fact, if you turn to the next short chapter, you'll get some pointers on how to improve continuously.

Very Important Points To Remember

✔ Emotion means appealing to what is human in your audience.

✔ Audiences usually think with their logical minds but act on emotion.

- ✔ Use an attention-grabber to let the audience know you are near the end.

- ✔ Keep the closing brief—no more than two minutes, otherwise the emotion will become sappy.

- ✔ Always include a farewell at the end of the presentation.

- ✔ Remain accessible to the audience until every member has left.

Fill in Your Favorite Tips from the Chapter

✔ _____
_____

✔ _____
_____

✔ _____
_____

✔ _____
_____

✔ _____
_____

✔ _____
_____

✔ _____
_____

✔ _____
_____

✔ _____
_____

✔ _____
_____

Close It Right!

This chapter reveals:

➤ How to improve your skills as a presenter

➤ How you, your audience, and others can help you

➤ Valuable reference information for more study

13

Continuous Improvement

JEARY THEORY ▬▬▬▬▬▬

The road to true success in any endeavor is the will to continually improve.

"The trouble with most of us is that we would rather be ruined by praise than saved by criticism."
— Dr. Norman Vincent Peale

Improving Your Skills

If you follow the simple tips and apply the concepts laid out in this book, you will become a more effective presenter—guaranteed! But if you're like me, you'll want to *continuously* improve. The key is practicing effectively. This chapter briefly outlines what you can do to help yourself and what your audience and others can do to help you improve. I have included a reference guide that includes periodicals, books, and even trainers in your area who can help you improve your presentation skills.

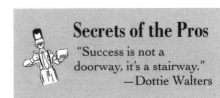

Secrets of the Pros

"Success is not a doorway, it's a stairway."
— Dottie Walters

What You Can Do

The first step is a commitment to continuous improvement. That means going after opportunities to present and continually rehearsing to improve your skills. It also means seeking and *listening* to constructive criticism. Detail will make or break a presentation. There's always some tweak you can make, some small something you can improve. Become dedicated to the process!

Evaluate yourself in any combination of the following ways:

➤ **Rehearse with a tape recorder or, better yet, a videotape.** If you get into this habit, you will eliminate surprises from your own presentations.

➤ **Consider new ways to accomplish the same job.** Experiment!

➤ **Present your next (or last) presentation in front of a mirror; then for a couple of friends; and finally before a large group.** This will give you a feel for how different presenting before different sizes of groups can be.

➤ **Fix *any* flaws—however small—before the next presentation.**

Be imaginative when it comes to improving yourself. Perhaps the most powerful tool discussed so far is the videotape. You may be the last person to know you're making a mistake. But to see yourself doing it over and over is a sure way to stop repeating errors.

Audience Evaluations

Audience evaluations are useful tools for improving your performance and gauging how effective a particular presentation has been. Additionally, these evaluations result in detailed information from the mind that matters most—that of the audience member. Videotapes

Secrets of the Pros

"The only true security in life comes from knowing that every single day you are improving yourself in some way."

—Anthony Robbins

are powerful for revealing the big picture, but audience evaluations provide a much more exacting level of detail. For optimal results, you should develop a detailed checklist and ask your audience's opinion. Design your checklist in the following manner:

➤ **Easy to use**

➤ **Specific**

➤ **Honest**

➤ **Comprehensive**

➤ **As brief as possible**

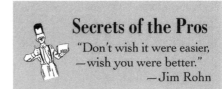

Secrets of the Pros

"Don't wish it were easier,
—wish you were better."
—Jim Rohn

As a rule, your forms should be no more than one page and should solicit information from a number of different areas of the presentation including:

➤ **The topics and content of the presentation**

➤ **The presenter's performance and preparation**

➤ **The materials used**

➤ **The effectiveness of visual aids**

➤ **Areas that need improvement**

➤ **Participation**

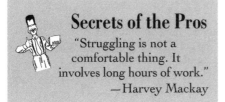

Secrets of the Pros

"Struggling is not a comfortable thing. It involves long hours of work."
—Harvey Mackay

You can use a checklist format, a 1–10 evaluative, or short-answer format. The object is to get as detailed a critique as possible from the audience. (Some sample evaluation forms follow on the next three pages, and I've repeated the forms in the appendix in the back of this book so you can remove them for photocopying.)

Prepare yourself. Audiences can be tough critics and even one tough review in a hundred will sting. But it will also help you improve. We're after 100 percent buy-in. When reviewing evaluations, remember *three* very important rules.

1. **The audience is always right.**

2. **The audience is always right.**

3. **The audience is always right.**

PRESENTATION ASSESSMENT

Skill/Traits	1	2	3	4	5	6	7	8	9	10

Preparation:

Analyzing audience — — — — — — — — — —

Developing objectives — — — — — — — — — —

Developing visual aids — — — — — — — — — —

Checking logistics — — — — — — — — — —

Overcoming nervousness — — — — — — — — — —

Stating main ideas — — — — — — — — — —

Deciding supporting
information — — — — — — — — — —

Creating an opener — — — — — — — — — —

Developing transitions — — — — — — — — — —

Structuring the main body — — — — — — — — — —

Using visual aids — — — — — — — — — —

Preparing the close — — — — — — — — — —

Delivery:

Vocal image

Volume — — — — — — — — — —

Pace — — — — — — — — — —

Pausing — — — — — — — — — —

Verbal image

Vocabulary — — — — — — — — — —

Grammar — — — — — — — — — —

Pronunciation — — — — — — — — — —

Visual image

Dress/appearance — — — — — — — — — —

Posture — — — — — — — — — —

Gestures — — — — — — — — — —

Eye contact — — — — — — — — — —

Facial expressions/smile — — — — — — — — — —

Challenging situations:

Handling questions — — — — — — — — — —

Managing mishaps — — — — — — — — — —

Controlling problem people — — — — — — — — — —

BODY LANGUAGE EVALUATION

Title _____ Name of Evaluator _____ Date _____

NOTE TO THE EVALUATOR: In this presentation, the speaker is concentrating on body language. He or she should use gestures, facial expressions, and other body movements that illustrate and enhance the verbal message. In evaluating this speech, focus on delivery rather than content. Use a rating scale of 1 to 10, where 1 represents unsatisfactory and 10 indicates outstanding.

Action	Rating	Comments
Preparation	1 2 3 4 5 6 7 8 9 10	_____
Organization	1 2 3 4 5 6 7 8 9 10	_____
Appearance	1 2 3 4 5 6 7 8 9 10	_____
Topic	1 2 3 4 5 6 7 8 9 10	_____
Manner	1 2 3 4 5 6 7 8 9 10	_____
Body movements	1 2 3 4 5 6 7 8 9 10	_____
Posture	1 2 3 4 5 6 7 8 9 10	_____
Gestures	1 2 3 4 5 6 7 8 9 10	_____
Eye contact	1 2 3 4 5 6 7 8 9 10	_____

POST-PRESENTATION EVALUATION

Instructions: Read each group and circle the number that most closely describes how effective the presentation was in each respective area. Use a rating scale of 1 to 10 in which 1 represents unsatisfactory and 10 indicates outstanding.

Preparation and Content

1.	Opening	1	2	3	4	5	6	7	8	9	10
2.	Content material	1	2	3	4	5	6	7	8	9	10
3.	Organization of material	1	2	3	4	5	6	7	8	9	10
4.	Clarity of objectives	1	2	3	4	5	6	7	8	9	10
5.	Visual aids	1	2	3	4	5	6	7	8	9	10
6.	Handouts	1	2	3	4	5	6	7	8	9	10
7.	Value of exercises	1	2	3	4	5	6	7	8	9	10
8.	Closing	1	2	3	4	5	6	7	8	9	10

Comments: _____

_____

Delivery

1.	Objectives met	1	2	3	4	5	6	7	8	9	10
2.	Explanation of main points	1	2	3	4	5	6	7	8	9	10
3.	Audience's attention	1	2	3	4	5	6	7	8	9	10
4.	Audience involvement	1	2	3	4	5	6	7	8	9	10
5.	Voice quality	1	2	3	4	5	6	7	8	9	10
6.	Nonverbal communication	1	2	3	4	5	6	7	8	9	10
7.	Questions directed to audience	1	2	3	4	5	6	7	8	9	10
8.	Answers to audience questions	1	2	3	4	5	6	7	8	9	10
9	Time management	1	2	3	4	5	6	7	8	9	10
10.	Feedback	1	2	3	4	5	6	7	8	9	10
11.	Speaker's listening skills	1	2	3	4	5	6	7	8	9	10
12.	Humor	1	2	3	4	5	6	7	8	9	10

Comments: _____

_____

Facilities

1.	Room	1	2	3	4	5	6	7	8	9	10
2.	Seating arrangement	1	2	3	4	5	6	7	8	9	10
3.	Acoustics	1	2	3	4	5	6	7	8	9	10
4.	Lighting	1	2	3	4	5	6	7	8	9	10
5.	Equipment	1	2	3	4	5	6	7	8	9	10

Comments: _____

_____

Avoid the temptation to take reviews personally and defend yourself. Audiences don't care why you do something—they only care whether or not it works. Of course, you will run into people who are wrong. The world is full of hostile, angry, or downright crazy people just waiting for the chance to rip into a speaker. But for the most part, people are just trying to be honest. Remember, you can even learn from a crank if you're willing to listen.

> ### Secrets of the Pros
> "One of the things that distinguishes masters from others is that they constantly ask for anything and everything they need. They ask for time, assistance, instruction, mentoring and coaching."
> —Jack Canfield and Mark Victor Hansen

What Outsiders Can Do

Seek critics. The best are those who have some training as presenters (or at least frequent listeners). This could include an associate, a coach, a colleague, a friend. Again, when people are criticizing you, ask for detailed critiques. Make sure critics comment on the following parts of your presentation:

➤ The delivery

➤ Your appearance and dress

➤ The "feel" of your performance

➤ Flaws of any kind

Again, *avoid the temptation to take things personally*. You're out to improve, so it's just business. In any case, you want your critics to be open and honest, not reluctant to give a frank evaluation because you might get mad!

On Work

The key ingredient to improvement is the will to improve, and after that comes work. You don't have to be a workaholic, a millionaire, a Ph.D., a genius, or even all that talented to improve. You just need the will to improve and the strength of character to listen to what can sometimes be unpleasant advice.

The fact that you've come to the end of this book proves you have the dedication. I believe you also have the character it takes to make it happen.

Secrets of the Pros

"What defines the few as the top is an uncommon stubbornness to accept 'the best' as the only viable choice."

—Bob Meintroup

The following pages consist of recommended resources that I hope will be of further value to you.

RECOMMENDED RESOURCES

ASSOCIATIONS

ASTD (AMERICAN SOCIETY FOR TRAINING AND DEVELOPMENT)
Association of trainers—mostly in-house corporate, some contract trainers and consultants. Most cities have monthly lunch or dinner meetings with speakers. Value: information, ideas, industry trends, networking contacts, annual training sessions locally and nationally. 1630 Duke Street, P. O. Box 1443, Alexandria, VA 22313. (703) 683-8100.

NSA (NATIONAL SPEAKERS ASSOCIATION)
Association of professional speakers—individuals, some well-known authors, primarily providing keynote speeches and shorter presentations. Most cities have monthly meetings with speakers. Valuable networking, ideas and information to shorten learning curve. National convention and regional meetings are worth attending. 3877 Seventh Street, Suite 350, Phoenix, AZ 85014. (602) 265-1001.

TOASTMASTERS INTERNATIONAL
The world's largest organization devoted to communication excellence. Through local clubs, Toastmasters offers you the opportunity to learn effective communication through practical experience. In other words, it is a non-profit, self-supporting group of individuals who meet on a regular basis to develop basic speaking skills. Various certifications are available, guided by manuals

provided by the national organization. Structure is very valuable, support is excellent. One of the best things you can do to increase your confidence in front of audiences. Very affordable, there is most likely a meeting group in your area. I attended weekly years ago when I entered this industry—and I recommend it highly. P. O. Box 9052, Mission Viejo, CA 92690. (714) 858-8255.

ISSAC (INTERNATIONAL SOCIETY OF SPEAKERS, AUTHORS, AND CONSULTANTS)

An international organization dedicated to expanding the careers, increasing the effectiveness, and enhancing the lives of speakers, authors, and consultants. P. O. Box 6432, Humble, TX 77525-6432. (800) 6-SPEAKER (677-3253).

SPEAKERS' & TRAINERS' BUREAUS

WALTERS INTERNATIONAL SPEAKERS BUREAU

Founded by Dottie Walters, a well-known and respected speaking expert. P. O. 1120, Glendora, CA 91740. Contact Lilly Walters at (818) 335-8069 or 1855.

HIGH PERFORMANCE RESOURCES

Founded by Tony Jeary, providing train-the-trainer services, career consultations and specialized training. HPR works primarily with large communication agencies matching the right people (speakers, trainers and consultants) to the right projects. 3001 LBJ Freeway, Suite 240, Dallas, TX 75234. Call Reg Cavender at (800) 982-2509.

MAGAZINES

Sharing Ideas, a top independent publication in the field of professional speaking. P. O. 1120, Glendora, CA 91740. (818) 335-8069 or 1855.

Training, a monthly publication focusing on the latest news, ideas, and technology for training adults. Lakewood Publications, 50 S. Ninth Street, Minneapolis, MN 55402.

Presentations, a monthly publication, focusing mostly on technology available for making presentations. Lakewood Publications, 50 S. Ninth Street, Minneapolis, MN 55402.

NEWSLETTERS

Inspire Any Audience Newsletter, produced by High Performance Resources, offers the reader updated information and tips on making powerful presentations. 3001 LBJ Freeway, Suite 240, Dallas, TX 75234. Call (972) 484-9627.

CATALOGS

Pfeiffer & Company International Publishers—They offer books, videos, and seminar kits for the human resources professionals and trainers.

Training Ideas: Resource Guide & Product Catalog (Talico Incorporated)—Offers a wide range of resources such as climate surveys, supervisory skill tests, training videos and books, training games and exercises, and more.

HRD Press—Aimed directly at the human resource development market, HRD Press offers workshop kits, games, computer-based training, books, videos, and more.

Recommended Resources (Lakewood Publications)—One of the most comprehensive collections of tools for training and presenting.

CRM Films, Video Training Resource—Offers a variety of video rental tapes on such subjects as decision making, customer service, empowerment, leadership, and more. High content, entertaining storylines, and each tape is accompanied by comprehensive instructional materials. They even offer free previews. Call for a free catalog: (800) 421-0833.

BOOKS

Flip Charts: How to Draw Them and How to Use Them, Richard Brandt (Pfeiffer & Company, ISBN 0-88390-031-9). A handbook of practical things that work when using flip charts. Easy to read and easy to use.

Creative Training Techniques, Robert Pike (Lakewood Publications, ISBN 0-94321-06-2). Bob Pike is well-known in the training industry as a leader when it comes to presentation creative input. He also holds fantastic seminars and publishes a great newsletter.

You've Got to be Believed to be Heard, Bert Decker (St. Martins Press, ISBN 0-312-09949-5). This very unique book is a must for the serious presenter who wants to increase audience buy-in and believability. Decker Communications offers a newsletter, tapes, and seminars.

Money Talks: The Complete Guide to Creating a Profitable Workshop or Seminar in Any Field, and *How to Make a Whole Lot More Than $1,000,000 Writing . . .,* Dr. Jeffrey Lant (Jeffrey Lant Associates, ISBN 0-940374-26-9). These books are packed with creative ideas to make money and improve your skills. Dr. Lant has a variety of other very useful books and special reports.

How to Get Your Point Across in 30 Seconds—or Less, Milo O. Frank (Simon & Schuster, ISBN 0-671-52492-5). The common ability of most efficient managers and leaders in every business and profession is the ability to present themselves and their ideas effectively. This book shows us how to make the most of every opportunity.

Secrets of Successful Speakers, Lilly Walters (McGraw-Hill, ISBN 0-07-068033-7). The title says it all. This book is full of ideas to help you take your next speech or presentation to the next level.

The Secrets of Charisma, Doe Lang (SPI Books, ISBN 0-944007-41-4). What is that intangible "something" that sets great leaders and presenters apart? Charisma! This book tells how to develop and use it. An audio is also available.

The Leader's Edge, Sandy Linver (Simon & Schuster, ISBN 0-684-80433-6). This book is not a "how-to" book—it is a "where to" book, about where communicate development can take you. You can contact Linver's company, Speakeasy, Inc.

The Greatest Speakers I Ever Heard, Dottie Walters (WRS, ISBN 1-56796-052-9). Dottie is one of the co-founders of the National Speakers Association and an incredible resource; be sure to get all of her books, tapes, and programs. Walters International Speakers Bureau, 18825 Hicreast Road, Glendale, CA 91741.

How to Make It Big in the Seminar Business, Paul Kavasik (McGraw-Hill, ISBN 0-07-033185-5). Paul has specialized in the seminar business, founding ASLA, the American Seminar Leaders Association. The seminar business is one of the most lucrative, glamorous, and prestigious entrepreneurial opportunities available in America today.

How to Have the Awesome Power of Public Speaking, Peter Daniels (House of Tabor, ISBN 0-949330-25-6). Peter Daniels outlines different areas of public speaking from the perspective of the speaker's power and responsibility with an audience.

How to Present Like a Pro, Lani Arredondo (McGraw-Hill, ISBN 0-07-002506-1). This is a practical guide for making persuasive presentations. It's basic premise: "Information alone doesn't persuade people; strong presentation skills do."

I Can See You Naked, Ron Hoff (Andrews & McMeel, ISBN 0-8362-8000-8).

Presentations Plus, David Peoples (John Wiley & Sons, ISBN 0-471-55956-3). Regardless of your audience, this book offers many useful strategies, guidelines, and principles you can use to present, persuade, and win.

You^2, Price Pritchett, Ph.D. (Quicksilver Press, ISBN 0-944002-04). Making a quantum leap—going from you to You^2—means accomplishing far more, in far less time, with only a fraction of the effort you've been giving. Price Pritchett introduces us to the power of taking quantum leaps in this booklet available from Pritchett & Associates, Inc.

The Quantum Leap Strategy, Price Pritchett, Ph.D. (Quicksilver Press, ISBN 0-944002-08-0). Price Pritchett has very effectively focused on a variety of small booklets which have positioned him in the marketplace as an expert. This booklet is the sequel to *You²* and further explains the unconventional set of behaviors that will bring you breakthrough performance by showing you how to make quantum leaps in productivity, quality, and overall performance. This booklet is also available from Pritchett & Associates, Inc.

5 Secrets to Personal Productivity, Hanks and Pulsipher (Franklin, ISBN 0-939817-05-5). You can find this little book at one of my favorite resources, Franklin Quest, the creator of the Franklin Day Planner. This book is to the point and very valuable if increasing your results is important to you.

How to Argue and Win Every Time, Gerry Spence (St. Martins Press, ISBN 0-312-11827-9). Gerry Spence is a courtroom attorney who has never lost a case. His premise is that presentation success is based on credibility.

Raving Fans, Blanchard and Bowles (Morris, ISBN 0-688-12316-3). Ken Blanchard, known for his phenomenal best-seller, *The One Minute Manager*, has done it again with *Raving Fans*. If you have not read it, you need to. Your raving fans are the key to your future business and success.

Training Managers to Train, Bro. Herman E. Zuccarolli, CSC (Crisp, ISBN 0-931961-43-2). Part of the Crisp Fifty-Minute™ Series, this book focuses on answering the question: How exactly does a manager prepare for, plan, present, and follow up on training programs designed to yield competent employees? Crisp has books and videos available in the Fifty-Minute™ Series.

Facilitation Skills for Team Leaders, Donald Hackett, Ph.D. and Charles L. Martin, Ph.D. (Crisp, ISBN 1-56052-199-6). Another in Crisp's Fifty-Minute™ Series, this book is a resource that will help people who are placed in the roles of facilitators build their skills to become more effective team leaders.

The Spellbinder's Gift, Og Mandino (Fawcett Columbine, ISBN 0-449-90690-6). Og Mandino is a treasure among authors, a writer who infuses human relationships with the energy of the divine, the light of the miraculous. In this book, he tells the story of a retired motivational speaker's agent and God's calling him back into the work he had done all of his life.

Speak and Grow Rich, Dottie Walters and Lilly Walters (Prentice Hall, ISBN 0-13-825803-1). In this book, Dottie and Lilly have included all the techniques and shortcuts that today's top speakers use to generate fees of up to $800,000 and more! Earl Nightingale calls this book ". . . a first-class book for budding speakers. It is also a first-class book for professional speakers . . . ."

What to Say When . . . You're Dying on the Platform, Lilly Walters (McGraw-Hill, ISBN 0-07-068039-6). Turn to this "First-Aid Kit" for the quips, "saver" lines, and practical preventive strategies that will rescue your speech from hecklers, equipment breakdown, late arrivals (including yours), loud noises, missing props, and more!

Powerful Presentation Skills, Debra Smith (Career Track Publications). This is a step-by-step workbook that walks you through the process of building a powerful presentation.

Even More Games Trainers Play, Edward E. Scannell and John W. Newstrom (McGraw-Hill, ISBN 0-07-046414-6). This is the fourth in a series of "Games Trainers Play" books. They are all full of hundreds of activities, brain-teasers, and games that will positively increase the effectiveness of your next presentation.

How to Speak Like a Pro, Leon Fletcher (Ballantine, ISBN 0-345-33427-2). This book offers step-by-step strategies for developing the confidence to speak well anywhere—from the boardroom to the PTA meeting.

Secrets of Successful Speakers, Lilly Walters (McGraw-Hill, ISBN 0-07-068033-7). Lilly Walters outlines 11 easy steps to mastering the secrets of the most successful speakers of our day.

Speaker's Sourcebook II, Glenn Van Ekeren (Prentice Hall, ISBN 0-13-825225-4). This is a unique collection of fresh and relevant stories and anecdotes that will delight any audience.

Speaking Magic, Carolyn Dickson (Oakhill Press, ISBN 0-9619590-8-8). This is a fast-reading book on the keys to taking control in front of an audience.

What to Say and How to Say It, David Belson (Citadel Press, ISBN 0-8065-1447-7). This handbook provides examples of things to say for the most frequent situations you face, such as weddings, retirements, dedications, birthdays, etc.

Endless Referrals, Bob Burg (McGraw-Hill, ISBN 0-07-008942-6). This is a great book on how to network your everyday contacts into sales and set yourself apart in today's sell-saturated world of junk, faxes and telemarketing.

See You at the Top, Zig Ziglar (Pelican Publishing, ISBN 0-88289-126-X). This is Zig's cornerstone book, just one of the twelve outstanding books he has written and one of the most influential books I've ever read.

AUDIO TAPES (ALBUMS)

Speak to Win, Bert Decker (Nightingale-Conant Corporation). Bert Decker covers the 12 areas of speaking in this six-cassette audio program.

The Complete Speaker, Earl Nightingale (Nightingale-Conant Corporation). This advanced, comprehensive six-cassette program covers every facet — in just about every possible situation — of public speaking.

The 7 Fee Ranges of the Speaking & Training Industry, Juanell Teague (People Plus). A powerful evaluation and planning tool to help determine what fees to charge to match your worth and protect your credibility.

WORKSHOP

Inspire Any Audience Workshop. An in-house customized workshop for six to fifty people. Contact High Performance Resources at (800) 982-2509.

PRODUCTS

Pierce Business Products provides an effective tool to help you make presentations in quality style. The Presenter flipchart easel helps you look professional by giving you the versatility and flexibility that you need to address any group effectively. This tool is featured on the back cover of the book. I have used one for years and highly recommend this tool to you. Call Pierce Business Products at (800) 372-7377 or write them at Three Bryan Drive, Wheeling, WV 26003.

The TUMI 243D 22-inch wheel-a-way is what I use as my trainer's toolbox. This is the best rolling bag I've owned. Contact TUMI Luggage, 250 Lackland Dr., Middlesex, NJ 08846. (908) 271-9500.

The laser pointer that I am holding in my hand on the front cover is by Lyte Optronics. This has become an invaluable part of my toolbox. Call Lyte Optronics at (310) 450-8551.

Mr. Sketch scented markers are the only choice for working with flip charts. The smell of traditional markers can literally make people ill. I buy these markers by the dozen to make me and my audience more comfortable during presentations. Call Sanford at (800) 438-3703.

Post-it™ Easel Pads and Easel Rolls help enhance communications in meetings and presentations. These pads, which are simply flipchart-sized Post-it™ notes, allow you to focus on the content of your meetings and are great for posting completed flipchart pages around the room without damaging walls or other surfaces. 3M Commercial Office Supply Division, P. O. Box 130514, Roseville, MN 55113-9759.

PEOPLE

Presentation Coaches can be reached by contacting Reg Cavender at (800) 982-2509.

John Bacon, Ann Arbor, Michigan

Sherry Boecher, Overland Park, Kansas

Judy Chaffee, Naperville, Illinois

Richard Clipp, Overland Park, Kansas

Fred Collins, Colleyville, Texas

Rick Davis, McKinney, Texas

Dave Freeborn, Simpsonville, South Carolina

Derek Green, Ann Arbor, Michigan

Myra Ketterman, Mountain Rest, South Carolina

Doug Kevorkian, Ann Arbor, Michigan

Lindsay Lowe, Marietta, Georgia

Bob Meintrup, Edwardsville, Illinois

Patrick O'Dooley, Dallas, Texas

Mark Pantak, Dallas, Texas

Steve Richards, Chamblee, Georgia

Tim Salladay, Bedford, Texas

Tony Walker, Overland Park, Kansas

Dale Ware, Houston, Texas

PROMOTIONS

The following pages contain promotions which I believe will be of special interest to you.

High Performance Resources, Inc.

3001 LBJ Freeway, Suite 240; Dallas, TX 75234 972.484.9627 • hprinfo@hprinc.com

High Performance Resources (HPR) is a valuable resource for training companies, training departments, and large communication agencies.

High Performance Resources excels in five (5) key functional areas:

- Program Ideas and Instructional Design
- Program Development (Curriculum/Meeting Leader Guides)
- Project Management
- Train-the-Trainer Projects (Cascade Training in any Language)
- Program Implementation (Delivery)

In addition to our full-time staff of professionals, we have long-term relationships and strategic alliances with hundreds of trainers, consultants and program developers who are dedicated to the high performance and productivity standards we demand and expect on behalf of our customers. A major strength is our flexibility, which allows us to work on a contract, joint-venture, or retainer basis to produce and develop the programs and assignments we accept from our clients.

Every project we accept receives the special attention of HPR professionals as we study and define the objectives of each project, whether it has a budget of $10,000 or $1,000,000. We focus on how to combine the internal resources of our client with our own staff and our extended staff of world-class consultants and contractors to produce excellent results, every time!

We have supported, initiated, managed, and delivered hundreds of training programs around the world including new product launches, sales training, and management training. We have also created and provided soft-skill programs on Teamwork, Customer Service, Presentations, and Communication. We have testimonials that consistently praise our ability to meet client objectives in a fashion that is unmatched by our competition. At HPR we focus on our clients' needs and producing results! We are driven to "get the job done" and our customers testify to our success.

Boost Your Performance With Zig Ziglar Training!

The Dallas, Texas-based Zig Ziglar Corporation offers curricula on sales performance, time management, customer service, change readiness, sales certification through the Dutch Council for Accreditation, RvA, (analogous to ISO 9000), personal development and numerous other subjects. The four core programs offered through *Ziglar Education Systems* include: Strategies For Success, Inspire Any Audience, Selling!, and Customer Service. Each is a video-based, instructor-led training program which is 12 to 14 hours in length; each can be taught in modular form.

Strategies For Success

The popular skills-based program, Strategies For Success, has helped thousands of people improve their personal and business lives. Audience members receive ethics training, wellness training, and stress management training all in one program. Topics covered: Foundations for success; the winner's attitude; developing excellence in self and others; and the goals formula.

Selling!

Designed to help sales or sales management professionals gain more confidence, competence and comfort in selling, this curriculum includes the following modules: The Psychology of Selling; The Prospect; The Product; The Process; Objections; and The Person. Featuring Bryan Flanagan, The Ziglar Director of Sales Training, Selling! will enable audience members to communicate more effectively to a wider range of prospects, use high-impact and high-gain questions, and more effectively assess sales skills to determine strengths and weaknesses.

Customer Service

Whatever your business, customers are watching you! Internal and external customers demand attention, satisfaction, value, and quality service. Customer Service covers the do's and don'ts of today's global customer competition, i.e., please a customer and impress them so much that they keep returning. Audience members learn the five basics of good telephone style; three different types of service; universal steps for resolving complaints; how to control customers' anger, and the importance of teamwork as related to Customer Service.

Inspire Any Audience

Based on the book you are holding in your hands, this curriculum is designed to assist business professionals in the art of presenting, an important experience that directly affects earning potential. Through six video-based modules, participants learn how to effectively prepare and develop a presentation; the correct use of body language; how to win the audience in the first three minutes; when visuals add impact; plus how to communicate with poise, power and assurance. This course is a must for the serious business professional!

Call 800-527-0306 Today!

This chapter includes:

➤ The Glossary of terms

➤ The Index

➤ The Appendix

➤ The Top Secrets from the book on tear-out cards for further study

14

Glossary
of Terms

Anecdote

A short story used during a presentation to illustrate or emphasize a point.

Articulation

Clear, concise formation of consonant and vowel sounds. Articulation results in speech that is easy for the audience to understand.

Audience

People that a presenter addresses. Can be one or more people. (See *Participants*.)

Body

The middle portion of a presentation. This section develops and supports the main concepts of thorough use of information, activities, and other material.

229

Body Language

Mannerisms or gestures used for the purpose of emphasizing a point. Studies show that success in a presentation depends about 7% on the words spoken, 38% on the tone of the words spoken and 55% on the body language of the speaker.

Business Entertainment™

The use of activities, games, or role-playing during a presentation to counter a short attention span. Usually, these activities are placed at five- to six-minute intervals.

Cliché

Standard phrases or comparisons that have become trite from overuse.

Communication

The social process of defining concepts and information through use of symbols. Can be written, verbal, or nonverbal.

Conclusion

Final section of a presentation during which main concepts are summarized and reemphasized.

Connotation

Attitude or emotion associated with a word; an overtone. (See *Denotation.*)

Continuous Improvement

Commitment to using audience feedback and other forms of criticism to continually improve presentation skills.

Credibility

A speaker's believability. A credible speaker is one who has the trust and confidence of the audience.

Culture

Traditions and lifestyles of a group of people.

Deductive Reasoning

A process of reasoning that bases conclusions on a general rule. Individual examples are explained and justified by the rule. (See *Inductive Reasoning.*)

Denotation

Literal dictionary meaning of a word; a word's definition.

Diaphragm

Muscle separating the chest from the abdomen. Control over this muscle results in improved breathing and speaking ability.

Empathic Listening

Listening that occurs when an audience identifies with a speaker and gives emotional support.

Evaluative Listening

A type of listening that results in a decision-making process.

Evidence

Facts, statistics, or any other form of data that supports a thesis.

Eye Contact

Making direct visual contact with members of the audience. Eye contact develops trust and credibility.

Facilitator

One who simplifies information so that the audience can easily understand concepts and relationships. Incorporates games, role-playing, and other interactive methods to involve the audience.

Feedback

Response of audience to presentation.

Four Audience Tensions

In every presentation, four sources of tension exist: audience to presenter, audience to environment, audience to audience, and audience to material.

Funneling

Processing of all possible presentation material to arrive at three major objectives that will be presented.

Identification

Ability of an audience to relate to presentation; perception that speaker is similar to them and trustworthy.

Impromptu Speaking

Speaking with little or no preparation and no notes.

Inductive Reasoning

Process of reasoning that uses specific examples to explain a general rule.

Infer

Using a generalization to imply a meaning.

Informative Presentation

Seeks to expand audience knowledge by defining concepts and relationships.

Inspire

Unique ability of a speaker to move an audience. Listeners not only hear words, but act on them.

Instructor

Speaker or presenter who provides information or instruction to an audience. May or may not use visual aids. May or may not use interactive methods.

Introduction

Beginning of a presentation. Section that states purpose and provides preview of material that will be covered.

Lecturer

Speaker or presenter who provides information to audience. Communication is, generally, one way.

Participants

In an interactive presentation, the audience members are referred to as participants. The term reflects the dynamic and interactive atmosphere that a presentation seeks to create.

Perception

Meaning given to the understanding of concepts. Generally, does not incorporate interactive method.

Persuasive Presentation

Presentation that seeks to move audience to particular action or belief.

Prejudice

Preconceived notion, opinion, or judgment regarding a person or group.

Presentation

Speaking to one or more people to present concepts and relationships in an interactive and dynamic manner.

Presenter

Presents material to audience, generally with use of visual aids and activities that involve the audience.

Public Communication

Communication with a large group. One person speaks as an audience listens.

Speaker

Delivers information while audience listens. Generally, audience participation is minimal.

Speech

Lecture-oriented means of delivering information.

Speech Communication

Sending and receiving oral messages for the purpose of creating meaning.

Subconscious Desires

Needs or wants that nearly all of us share. They include: to belong, to be respected, to be liked, to be safe, to succeed, to find romance, to be inspired.

Targeted Polling

Means of monitoring individual audience responses. Seeking feedback from particular individuals.

Testimonial

Endorsement of person, place, or thing. Usually, celebrities are used.

Trainer

Trains audience to perform a skill. Usually, through hands-on practice.

Verbal Survey

Method of monitoring audience response during a presentation.

Visual Aid

Any audio or visual aid to a presentation. Charts, maps, graphs, tapes, movies, overhead projections, slides, and flip charts are common visual aids.

Index

Index

Index

Index

APPENDIX
Reproducible Pages

AUDIENCE WORKSHEET

What sort of knowledge about my topic do they bring to the table?

_____

_____

_____

Will they be for me or against me? Why?

_____

_____

_____

List of people whom they admire in their organization and are most likely to admire outside of it:

_____

_____

_____

Things that have worked with similar audiences in the past—and things that haven't:

_____

_____

_____

Why was I asked to present?

_____

_____

THE PRESENTATION WORK ORDER

Title of Presentation _____

Date of Presentation _____

How much time do I have to prepare? _____

How much time will I have to speak? _____

What kind of room will I be speaking in?

❑ Conference room   ❑ Living room

❑ Boardroom   ❑ Other _____

❑ Classroom

How many people will I be speaking to? _____

What type of financial budget is available?

❑ Large budget—lots of money, as in   <u>$ Let's do it right!</u>
    "Money is no (big) object."

❑ Small budget—money is available $ _____
    but is definitely an object.

❑ No budget—money isn't an object $ _____0_____
    because there's none to spend.

What type of equipment will be available to me?

❑ Flip chart(s)?   ❑ Overhead projector?

❑ Tape player?   ❑ VCR and monitor?

❑ Advanced presentation   ❑ Chairs and tables?
    hardware and software?

❑ Other _____

What type of equipment do I need to provide/rent?_____
_____

3D OUTLINE™

Title of Presentation: _____

Objectives:

- _____
- _____
- _____

Time	Who	What	Why	How

CHECKLIST FOR EFFECTIVE REHEARSAL

Well before your presentation:

Prepare and mentally walk through:

❏ 3-D Outline™

❏ Each section of presentation

❏ 3x5 cards

Rehearse in front of :

❏ Other people

❏ Video camera

❏ Mirror

Just before your presentation:

Locate and know how to operate
the following fixtures:

❏ Electrical outlets

❏ Lighting controls

❏ Volume controls for room sound

Locate the following:

❏ Restrooms

❏ Telephones

❏ Stairs and elevators

Comments:

_____

_____

_____

_____

_____

_____

_____

PRESENTATION ASSESSMENT

Skill/Traits	1	2	3	4	5	6	7	8	9	10

Preparation:

   Analyzing audience — — — — — — — — — —

   Developing objectives — — — — — — — — — —

   Developing visual aids — — — — — — — — — —

   Checking logistics — — — — — — — — — —

   Overcoming nervousness — — — — — — — — — —

   Stating main ideas — — — — — — — — — —

   Deciding supporting information — — — — — — — — — —

   Creating an opener — — — — — — — — — —

   Developing transitions — — — — — — — — — —

   Structuring the main body — — — — — — — — — —

   Using visual aids — — — — — — — — — —

   Preparing the close — — — — — — — — — —

Delivery:

   Vocal image

     Volume — — — — — — — — — —

     Pace — — — — — — — — — —

     Pausing — — — — — — — — — —

   Verbal image

     Vocabulary — — — — — — — — — —

     Grammar — — — — — — — — — —

     Pronunciation — — — — — — — — — —

   Visual image

     Dress/Appearance — — — — — — — — — —

     Posture — — — — — — — — — —

     Gestures — — — — — — — — — —

     Eye contact — — — — — — — — — —

     Facial expressions/Smile — — — — — — — — — —

Challenging situations:

   Handling questions — — — — — — — — — —

   Managing mishaps — — — — — — — — — —

   Managing problem people — — — — — — — — — —

BODY LANGUAGE EVALUATION

Title _____ Name of Evaluator _____ Date _____

NOTE TO THE EVALUATOR: In this presentation the speaker is concentrating on body language. He or she should use gestures, facial expressions, and other body movements that illustrate and enhance the verbal message. In evaluating this speech, focus on delivery rather than content. Use a rating scale of 1 to 10, where 1 represents unsatisfactory and 10 indicates outstanding.

Action	Rating	Comments
Preparation	1 2 3 4 5 6 7 8 9 10	_____
Organization	1 2 3 4 5 6 7 8 9 10	_____
Appearance	1 2 3 4 5 6 7 8 9 10	_____
Topic	1 2 3 4 5 6 7 8 9 10	_____
Manner	1 2 3 4 5 6 7 8 9 10	_____
Body movements	1 2 3 4 5 6 7 8 9 10	_____
Posture	1 2 3 4 5 6 7 8 9 10	_____
Gestures	1 2 3 4 5 6 7 8 9 10	_____
Eye contact	1 2 3 4 5 6 7 8 9 10	_____
Facial expressions	1 2 3 4 5 6 7 8 9 10	_____

POST-PRESENTATION EVALUATION

Instructions: Read each group and circle the number that most closely describes how effective the presentation was in each respective area. Use a rating scale of 1 to 10 in which 1 represents unsatisfactory and 10 indicates outstanding.

Preparation and Content

1.	Opening	1	2	3	4	5	6	7	8	9	10
2.	Content material	1	2	3	4	5	6	7	8	9	10
3.	Organization of material	1	2	3	4	5	6	7	8	9	10
4.	Clarity of objectives	1	2	3	4	5	6	7	8	9	10
5.	Visual aids	1	2	3	4	5	6	7	8	9	10
6.	Handouts	1	2	3	4	5	6	7	8	9	10
7.	Value of exercises	1	2	3	4	5	6	7	8	9	10
8.	Closing	1	2	3	4	5	6	7	8	9	10

Comments: _____

_____

Delivery

1.	Objectives met	1	2	3	4	5	6	7	8	9	10
2.	Explanation of main points	1	2	3	4	5	6	7	8	9	10
3.	Audience's attention	1	2	3	4	5	6	7	8	9	10
4.	Audience involvement	1	2	3	4	5	6	7	8	9	10
5.	Voice quality	1	2	3	4	5	6	7	8	9	10
6.	Nonverbal communication	1	2	3	4	5	6	7	8	9	10
7.	Questions directed to audience	1	2	3	4	5	6	7	8	9	10
8.	Answers to audience questions	1	2	3	4	5	6	7	8	9	10
9	Time management	1	2	3	4	5	6	7	8	9	10
10.	Feedback	1	2	3	4	5	6	7	8	9	10
11.	Speaker's listening skills	1	2	3	4	5	6	7	8	9	10
12.	Humor	1	2	3	4	5	6	7	8	9	10

Comments: _____

_____

Facilities

1.	Room	1	2	3	4	5	6	7	8	9	10
2.	Seating arrangement	1	2	3	4	5	6	7	8	9	10
3.	Acoustics	1	2	3	4	5	6	7	8	9	10
4.	Lighting	1	2	3	4	5	6	7	8	9	10
5.	Equipment	1	2	3	4	5	6	7	8	9	10

Comments: _____

_____

**Zig Ziglar
& Tony Jeary**

Announce New Training

The Zig Ziglar Corporation is pleased to announce a new, video-supported program of training developed for Ziglar Education Systems in connection with international presentation coach, Tony Jeary, of High Performance Resources, Incorporated. The new curriculum consists of interactive training which will teach participants how to be well-versed presenters, and how to create and develop a convincing presentation of any kind.

Jeary is the author of *Inspire Any Audience: Proven Secrets of the Pros for Powerful Presentations,* the book which is the basis for the Ziglar training program, appropriately named *Inspire Any Audience.* Following the format of three other successful Ziglar programs (Customer Service, Strategies For Success, and Selling!) *Inspire Any Audience* consists of six videos, a leader's guide, and a student workbook. Sessions are a total of twelve to fourteen hours, and can be abbreviated into segments to fit whatever format a client desires.

Participants in this Ziglar training will learn the use of body language; steps to control nervousness; when visuals add impact; plus tried-and-tested methods on how to communicate with poise, power, and assurance. Modules include: *What To Do Before a Presentation; How To Effectively Prepare And Develop A Presentation; Winning In The First Three Minutes; The Key Skills That Make Any Presentation Shine; Mastering The Tools Of The Trade; and Summarzing And Closing A Presentation.*

For further information on *Inspire Any Audience* and other Ziglar products & services, contact The Zig Ziglar Corporation (800) 527-0306 • 3330 Earhart Drive, Carrollton, TX 75006.

Master the art of presentation!

In this video-based modular course, you can learn to prepare in half the time!

MODULE 1
What To Do Before A Presentation

- Learn professional presentation skills; begin with the elements that make a presentation "work"
- Clarify the objective(s) of your presentation; establish audience profile
- Understand your audience's seven subconscious desires
- Determine the four categories of audience members and the attributes of each group
- Master the "Funneling Process" for creating effective presentations

MODULE 2
How To Effectively Prepare And Develop A Presentation

- Create a presentation from scratch; save valuable time in preparation
- Build a 3-D Outline™ for organizing your presentation quickly
- Learn rehearsal techniques for flawless presenting
- Understand six main components from segments to summaries; determine components of presentation excellence

MODULE 3
Winning In The First 3 Minutes

- Gain instant credibility; learn proactive steps to control nervousness
- Implement rapport-building to win a favorable first impression
- Understand the "Four Audience Tensions" and how to reduce them
- Employ "hooks" for undivided attention; get a collection of sure openers for success
- Apply 12 Commandments for building and maintaining rapport; ensure your acceptance

MODULE 4
The Key Skills That Make Any Presentation Shine

- Learn and implement effective body language, i.e., facial gestures, eye contact, hand movements
- Understand "trust transference" and why it's vitally important
- Learn the secrets of Business Entertainment™ (fun factor); enjoy the benefit of repeat engagements
- Discover the key do's and don'ts of answering questions; learn to manage unexpected questions

MODULE 5
Measuring the Tools Of The Trade

- Learn how to use visual aids to increase retention; become a star performer
- Practice with various tools, i.e., props, video equipment, overheads, flip charts, handouts, music players, etc.
- Understand how to select appropriate tools for appropriate topics; gain comfort and confidence

MODULE 6
Summary And Closing The Presentation

- Discover the difference between summarizing and closing
- Determine how to summarize throughout the presentation for a power-packed ending
- Implement proper use of emotion for audience buy-in at closing
- Learn how to ensure audience member action after the presentation is over; become a presenter worth remembering

You'll learn how to get 100% audience buy-in so people will take action as a result of your presentations.

A Message from the Author

Dear Reader,

It is my sincere hope that the information presented in this book has been valuable to you. I believe with all my heart that our skill as presenters and communicators is a critical factor in our personal success formula, and my main objective is to help others become more successful in their professional efforts.

I am constantly seeking better ways to teach and train people to improve their presentation and communication skills. Therefore, I would really appreciate any comments or suggestions you have about the book. I invite you to write to me and share your thoughts. What are the best and most effective parts of the book? How could I have said things better? What could be added to make the book even more effective?

Write to: 3001 LBJ Freeway, Suite 240, Dallas, TX 75234
Fax: (800) 605-0765
E-Mail: MrPresentation@HPRinc.com

In addition, I have a powerful desire for this information to reach as many people as possible, and I know that nothing is more effective than a strong recommendation from a "satisfied customer." Would you be willing to help me spread the message of *Inspire Any Audience*? If so, you will be helping them become more successful, while experiencing a great reward in their thanks and appreciation.

During the next several months you *will* have the opportunity to tell *at least 10 others* about this book.

They might be personal friends, family members, or professional associates. You might know a CEO or business owner who could benefit their organization by learning the techniques presented in this book. Obviously, I am interested in selling more books, but my primary motive is to help others. You can help me accomplish that through your willingness to tell others about *Inspire Any Audience*.

I hope to hear from you soon. If you write to me, I will send you a free gift, so please include your return address.

Kindest regards,

Tony Jeary

About the Author

Congratulations! You have in your hands one of the finest tools available to help you improve your presentation skills. Since 1986, Tony Jeary has steadily increased his stature as a leading authority on presentation skills and is now known as "Mr. Presentation." He has included in this book specific, proven techniques designed to help you *Inspire Any Audience*.

Tony Jeary has helped educate and train thousands of people around the world and is regularly sought by major corporations to plan, develop, and facilitate training programs for their employees and associates. Jeary loves to coach, and train others to become powerful presenters and public speakers. This book is the result of his many years of experience in this field.

Tony has served as director of training for two large corporations during the past ten years and today is President and CEO of High Performance Resources (HPR), based in Dallas, Texas, with branch offices in Detroit, Los Angeles, and Taipei. HPR is an international training and consulting firm. Its clients include Chrysler Corporation, Ross Roy Communications, and the Zig Ziglar Corporation.

Tony believes that presentation and communication skills serve as a foundation for personal success and has written this book to help you begin to master this critical skill. Even if you are already a skilled presenter, you will quickly see that Tony Jeary is a master of presentation design. He uses the techniques he sets forth to clarify objectives and help construct the very best mix of information that can be delivered in any speech, training program, or general presentation.

Tony lives by the motto, "Give value. Do more than expected." Having been raised in an entrepreneurial family, he embraced this idea at a young age and reinforced it throughout his business career as he started, bought, and/or operated more than thirty businesses. Tony has spent his life cultivating special relationships through outstanding performance and helping other people meet their personal goals. This book is evidence of that creed and Tony's personal commitment to help others. It contains a lifetime of valuable tools and secrets that will assist you in your goal of personal or business success, as you learn how to *Inspire Any Audience*.

Contact High Performance Resources to bring Tony into your organization or for information on scheduling and licensing of corporate training programs.

High Performance Resources, Inc., 3001 LBJ Freeway, Suite 240, Dallas, TX 75234.
Phone: (972) 484-9627 or (800) 982-2509. Fax: (800) 605-0765.
EMail: MrPresentation@HPRinc.com

Presentation Development Secrets

1. Determine and clarify three primary objectives.
2. Define your limitations…
   - How much time do you have to prepare? To speak?
   - What kind of room will you be in?
   - How large is the budget you have to work with?
   - What equipment will be available?
3. Build a "3-D Outline™."
4. Apply a logical "sequence" to your presentation.
5. Pare back any point that takes more than 15 minutes to cover.
6. Identify and obtain any presentation aid (overheads, video, audio, props, etc.) that your budget will allow.
7. Always brainstorm and review your material with others.

Keys to Your First Three Minutes

1. Show respect and build rapport.
   - Make the audience your partner by asking their opinion
   - Prove you respect their time
   - Prove you are prepared
   - Show the audience how you are like them
   - Use eye contact
2. Grab the audience's attention; once you have it, *run with it!*
   - Use an "attention-grabber" opening
   - Avoid the four sure ways to KILL an opening:
     - ➤ An apology ➤ An unrelated/inappropriate anecdote
     - ➤ Equipment failure ➤ Long or slow-moving statements
   - Get your audience to commit to involvement

Meeting and Exceeding Expectations

1. Give value — do more than is expected!
2. Learn and use people's names.
3. Always think, "Why is my audience here?"
4. Establish expectations early in the presentation.
5. Create winning opportunities for your audience.
6. Always prepare more information than you think you'll need.
7. Your enthusiasm makes it easier for the audience to follow you.
8. Be flexible!

"Funneling Process"
(For Determining Presentation Objectives)

1. **Determine the action.**
2. **Define your audience.**
3. **Brainstorm to determine…**
   - Your needs
   - Your audience's needs
   - Any "third party" needs
4. **Select 3 or 4 written objectives.**
5. **Test your objectives mentally.**

3 CORE OBJECTIVES

Steps for Going from Nervous to Natural

1. Be confident about what you're talking about. — Practice thoroughly, the same way you'll actually deliver your presentation.
2. Be yourself. — Use your own natural speaking style. Do not try to be someone you're not.
3. Psyche yourself up. — "Positive Self-Talk," visualize success.
4. Work with your body's physical reaction to nerves:
   - Stretch; do some isometric exercises
   - Take deep breaths
   - Use the power of pausing
5. Bond with your audience. — Pick two or three friendly faces and speak to them. Feed off their positive energy.

Setting the Tone

1. Tone refers to more than just your "tone of voice."
   - The "feel" of the event creates an atmosphere
   - Details are important. Big things count, little things count
2. Big Things
   - Atmosphere = Emotion!
   - Create a conversation with your audience.
   - Remember "Tonometer" (tone spectrum).
   - Rate your own presentations!
3. A lot of little details that are really big details.
   - Eye contact
   - Enthusiasm
   - Appearance
   - Humor
   - Body language
   - Breaks
   - Word choice
   - Music
   - "Openness"

7 "Foundation Secrets" of Successful Presentations

1. Use the five-step "Funneling Process" to identify objectives.
2. Alleviate the four "Audience Tensions":
   - Other audience members
   - Instructor
   - Materials/handouts
   - Environment
3. Use "Trust Transference" to gain 100% buy-in.
4. Use "Business Entertainment™" to make the presentation fun.
5. Use "Verbal Surveying" to get constant audience feedback.
6. Use "Targeted Polling" to single out participant feedback.
7. Provide "Audience Closure" to guarantee that audience expectations were met/exceeded.

Rehearsing Your Presentation

1. Mentally walk through your presentation using a 3-D Outline™/Matrix.
2. Use 3 x 5 cards (of key points, timing, directions, etc.) while rehearsing.
3. Whenever possible, audio or videotape your practice sessions.
4. Rehearse in front of someone (associate, spouse, friend).
5. Rehearse with the equipment you'll be using (pointer, flip chart, overheads). Leave nothing to chance.
6. Walk the room before your presentation.
7. Sit in your audience's seats to get a feel from their perspective.

Being Credible

1. Credibility is established by the way you:
   - Demonstrate knowledge
   - Speak about experiences
   - Demonstrate preparedness
   - Demonstrate enthusiasm
2. Tell the truth.
   - Commit and adhere to a time requirement
   - Whenever you say you will do something, *follow through!*
3. Tell your audience why you have the right to be there.
   - A more relevant introduction means higher credibility
   - Share personal experiences to qualify with your audience
4. Connect with the audience.
   - Be natural
   - Be enthusiastic
   - Work the room
   - Be spontaneous
   - Be sincere

Presenter's Tool Box

- Pointers (laser and antennae type)
- "Scented" markers
- Name tags / blank 3 x 5 cards
- Camera
- Whistle
- Blank overhead transparencies
- Masking tape
- Surgical tape (for flip charts)
- White out
- Scissors
- Push pins
- Hole punch
- Tape measure
- Paper clips
- Rubber bands
- String
- Batteries
- Ruler

Tools

1. Locate the presentation room and double-check the following:
   - Sound system
   - Temperature controls
   - Electrical outlets/light switches
2. Set up props early.
3. Always use visual aids whenever possible.
4. Microphones—know them/use them.
5. "Rehearse" with and test equipment just as you rehearse yourself.

Closing

1. Use emotion to maximize the last few moments.
2. "Closing Killers" to avoid:
   - Questions and Answers
   - Apologizing
   - Admitting that something was missed
   - Skipping the summary
   - Rambling on
3. Paint a picture of the future challenge and motivate your audience to take action.

Summarizing

1. Link the body of your presentation to the introduction.
   - Tie the entire presentation together
2. Prove that you met the objectives you established in the beginning.
   - Administer/distribute evaluations
3. Provide closure for your audience.

Visual Aids (continued)

- Use pictures instead of sentence fragments.
- Combine pictures, symbols, and key words.
- Children's coloring books are a good source for pictures and drawings.
- Make visuals colorful.
- Use graphics related to the subject matter.

Keeping Their Attention

1. Understand that people think four times faster than we speak.
2. "Business Entertainment" enhances learning. Use these tools:
   - Music
   - Games
   - Stories
   - Videos
   - Breaks – intermission
   - Tone of voice
   - Gifts/Giveaways

Managing Your Presentation

1. Always strive for 100% Buy-in.
   - General—"Verbal Surveying"
   - Individual—"Targeted Polling"
2. Audience "Conscience Attention Units" always work to increase audience CAU.
3. Handling Questions.
   - If you don't know, say so and find out.
   - If the question is hostile, defer it to a break.
   - Involve your audience and ask if other audience members know.
4. Facilitation.

Visual Aids

- Keep visuals simple.
- Keep visuals legible.
- Keep visuals neat.
- Keep visuals consistent.
- Keep visuals unified.
- Use bulleted points and sentence fragments instead of full sentences.

Evaluations

1. Evaluate to ensure that you:
   - Satisfy your client
   - Provide information that will help you with future presentations and improve you as a presenter
2. Use (H.U.H.Y.) cards

7 "Foundation Secrets" of Successful Presentations

1. Use the five-step "Funneling Process" to identify objectives.
2. Alleviate the four "Audience Tensions":
   - Other audience members
   - Instructor
   - Materials/handouts
   - Environment
3. Use "Trust Transference" to gain 100% buy-in.
4. Use "Business Entertainment" to make the presentation fun.
5. Use "Verbal Surveying" to get constant audience feedback.
6. Use "Targeted Polling" to single out participant feedback.
7. Provide "Audience Closure" to guarantee that audience expectations were met/exceeded.

Rehearsing Your Presentation

1. Mentally walk through your presentation using a 3-D Outline™/Matrix.
2. Use 3 x 5 cards (of key points, timing, directions, etc.) while rehearsing.
3. Whenever possible, audio or videotape your practice sessions.
4. Rehearse in front of someone (associate, spouse, friend).
5. Rehearse with the equipment you'll be using (pointer, flip chart, overheads). Leave nothing to chance.
6. Walk the room before your presentation.
7. Sit in your audience's seats to get a feel from their perspective.

Being Credible

1. Credibility is established by the way you:
   - Demonstrate knowledge
   - Demonstrate preparedness
   - Speak about experiences
   - Demonstrate enthusiasm
2. Tell the truth.
   - Commit and adhere to a time requirement
   - Whenever you say you will do something, *follow through!*
3. Tell your audience why you have the right to be there.
   - A more relevant introduction means higher credibility
   - Share personal experiences to quality with your audience
4. Connect with the audience.
   - Be natural
   - Work the room
   - Be sincere
   - Be enthusiastic
   - Be spontaneous

"Funneling Process"
(For Determining Presentation Objectives)

1. Determine the action.
2. Define your audience.
3. Brainstorm to determine…
   - Your needs
   - Your audience's needs
   - Any "third party" needs
4. Select 3 or 4 written objectives.
5. Test your objectives mentally.

3 CORE OBJECTIVES

Steps for Going from Nervous to Natural

1. Be confident about what you're talking about. – Practice thoroughly, the same way you'll actually deliver your presentation.
2. Be yourself. – Use your own natural speaking style. Do not try to be someone you're not.
3. Psyche yourself up. – "Positive Self-Talk," visualize success.
4. Work with your body's physical reaction to nerves:
   - Stretch; do some isometric exercises
   - Take deep breaths
   - Use the power of pausing
5. Bond with your audience. – Pick two or three friendly faces and speak to them. Feed off their positive energy.

Setting the Tone

1. Tone refers to more than just your "tone of voice."
   - The "feel" of the event creates an atmosphere
   - Details are important. Big things count, little things count
2. Big Things
   - Atmosphere = Emotion!
   - Create a conversation with your audience.
   - Remember "Tonometer" (tone spectrum).
   - Rate your own presentations!
3. A lot of little details that are really big details.
   - Eye contact
   - Humor
   - Word choice
   - Enthusiasm
   - Body language
   - Music
   - Appearance
   - Breaks
   - "Openness"

Presentation Development Secrets

1. Determine and clarify three primary objectives.
2. Define your limitations…
   - How much time do you have to prepare? To speak?
   - What kind of room will you be in?
   - How large is the budget you have to work with?
   - What equipment will be available?
3. Build a "3-D Outline™."
4. Apply a logical "sequence" to your presentation.
5. Pare back any point that takes more than 15 minutes to cover.
6. Identify and obtain any presentation aid (overheads, video, audio, props, etc.) that your budget will allow.
7. Always brainstorm and review your material with others.

Keys to Your First Three Minutes

1. Show respect and build rapport.
   - Make the audience your partner by asking their opinion
   - Prove you respect their time
   - Prove you are prepared
   - Show the audience how you are like them
   - Use eye contact
2. Grab the audience's attention; once you have it, *run with it!*
   - Use an "attention-grabber" opening
   - Avoid the four sure ways to KILL an opening:
     ➤ An apology   ➤ An unrelated/inappropriate anecdote
     ➤ Equipment failure   ➤ Long or slow-moving statements
   - Get your audience to commit to involvement

Meeting and Exceeding Expectations

1. Give value—do more than is expected!
2. Learn and use people's names.
3. Always think, "Why is my audience here?"
4. Establish expectations early in the presentation.
5. Create winning opportunities for your audience.
6. Always prepare more information than you think you'll need.
7. Your enthusiasm makes it easier for the audience to follow you.
8. Be flexible!

Keeping Their Attention

1. Understand that people think four times faster than we speak.
2. "Business Entertainment" enhances learning. Use these tools:
   - Music
   - Games
   - Stories
   - Videos
   - Breaks – intermission
   - Tone of voice
   - Gifts/Giveaways

Managing Your Presentation

1. Always strive for 100% Buy-in.
   - General—"Verbal Surveying"
   - Individual—"Targeted Polling"
2. Audience "Conscience Attention Units" always work to increase audience CAU.
3. Handling Questions.
   - If you don't know, say so and find out.
   - If the question is hostile, defer it to a break.
   - Involve your audience and ask if other audience members know.
4. Facilitation.

Evaluations

1. Evaluate to ensure that you:
   - Satisfy your client
   - Provide information that will help you with future presentations and improve you as a presenter
2. Use (H.U.H.Y.) cards

Tools

1. Locate the presentation room and double-check the following:
   - Sound system
   - Temperature controls
   - Electrical outlets/light switches
2. Set up props early.
3. Always use visual aids whenever possible.
4. Microphones—know them/use them.
5. "Rehearse" with and test equipment just as you rehearse yourself.

Summarizing

1. Link the body of your presentation to the introduction.
   - Tie the entire presentation together
2. Prove that you met the objectives you established in the beginning.
   - Administer/distribute evaluations
3. Provide closure for your audience.

Visual Aids

- Keep visuals simple.
- Keep visuals legible.
- Keep visuals neat.
- Keep visuals consistent.
- Keep visuals unified.
- Use bulleted points and sentence fragments instead of full sentences.

Presenter's Tool Box

- Pointers (laser and antennae type)
- "Scented" markers
- Name tags/blank 3 x 5 cards
- Camera
- Whistle
- Blank overhead transparencies
- Masking tape
- Surgical tape (for flip charts)
- White out
- Scissors
- Push pins
- Hole punch
- Tape measure
- Paper clips
- Rubber bands
- String
- Batteries
- Ruler

Closing

1. Use emotion to maximize the last few moments.
2. "Closing Killers" to avoid:
   - Questions and Answers
   - Apologizing
   - Admitting that something was missed
   - Skipping the summary
   - Rambling on
3. Paint a picture of the future challenge and motivate your audience to take action.

Visual Aids (continued)

- Use pictures instead of sentence fragments.
- Combine pictures, symbols, and key words.
- Children's coloring books are a good source for pictures and drawings.
- Make visuals colorful.
- Use graphics related to the subject matter.